Theater
Games
For
Rehearsal

Viola Spolin

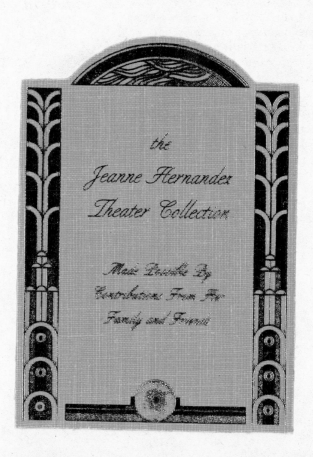

Theater Games For Rehearsal

A Director's Handbook

Viola Spolin

Northwestern
University
Press

Evanston, Illinois
1985

Published by Northwestern University Press
Evanston, Illinois 60201

ISBN #0-8101-4002-2 cloth, 4001-0 Paper
Library of Congress Catalog Card Number 85-60927

Printed in USA

Second Printing, 1988

CONTENTS

Dedication

To my sisters, Pauline Hirzel, Irene Norton, Beatrice Lees.

Acknowledgments

Thank you Carol Sills for your close work with me in the editing and typing of the manuscript and to my dear husband Kolmus Greene for your evaluations. Thank you Robert Martin. Thank you Paul Thompson of Northwestern University Press.

Preface

This work is intended to give the theater director a secure way of rehearsing a successful production through sidecoaching my theater games, which were originally developed as simple exercises for directing players working with a written script. Over the years my continuing development of the games provided an important rehearsal technique for improvisational groups throughout the world.

For children's and community groups the exercises began as ways of resolving production problems. These theatrical problems included the representation of character and emotion and the use of language and stage conventions as related to the written script the group was working on. EXITS AND ENTRANCES, p. 77, GIVE AND TAKE, p. 35, STAGE PICTURE, p. 40, BEGIN AND END, p. 46, GIBBERISH, p. 53, and many more games evolved during the weekly workshops that were held. As the value of play and playing became increasingly apparent, the word "game" displaced "problem-solving." Notes on techniques, motives, etc., became unnecessary. The logical, rational brain seeking such information had been transcended by the theater game focus.

Two scenes! Give and take! Stage picture! — these sidecoaching phrases and many others are your tools for directing your players. The meaning and purpose of these directives will become clear through continued use during workshops and rehearsals. Playing together in this manner brings all players into the same space no matter how diverse their backgrounds or training.

It cannot be emphasized too strongly that playing can pull many a director and cast out of a tight spot, freeing all of them from the fear-producing trap of memorizing, characterizing, and interpreting. This playing draws upon a very important, almost forgotten, little understood or utilized, and greatly maligned life-giving force — *passion!*

☐ *I discovered that during playing I could continue giving direction without stopping what the actors were doing. My direction then began to consist of sidecoaching the focus of the game when needed. Cluttered stages, for instance, were cleared by my calling out,* **Share the stage picture!**

☐ *The theater game focus awakens the intuitive.*

☐ *"In Spolin exercises, far from being beholden to theories, systems, techniques or laws, the actor becomes the artisan of his own [theater] education, which is produced freely of itself,"* Ingrid Dormien Koudela, *translator of the author's* Improvisation for the Theater, *in her introduction to the Brazilian edition.*

Chapter 1:
PREPARATION

Acting requires presence. Being there. Playing produces this state. Just as ballplayers in any sport are present in the playing, so must all theater members be present in the moment of playing, in present time.

Presence is a word that has unfortunately become overused. We all use it and think we know what it means. Often we sense it in another; occasionally we feel we achieve it, but we do not always know how to find and keep it.

Presence arrives through the intuitive. We cannot approach the intuition until we are free of opinions, attitudes, prejudices, and judgments. The very act of seeking the moment, of being open to fellow players, produces a life force, a flow, a regeneration for all who participate.

How can this come about? To begin with, a group (community) must be formed. All members, one hopes, come to the first rehearsal open to the script, the emerging event around which the community will form. As individuals we are isolated from one another, full of limitations, fears, tensions, competitiveness, prejudices, and preconceived attitudes. If our openness is more than just a hope, a sentiment, a word, certain conditions must be met. The first of these we would call mutuality or trust. True playing will produce trust.[1]

All who will work on a script must be free of the subjective thoughts underlying and/or connected with the very words as they are being spoken. This is accomplished by shutting off the words' power (which lies in *remembered* meaning and significance — old scenarios which rarely see what the eye sees, listen to what the ear hears, or know what the touch feels). Instead, one must enter the physiological, the very physical language itself, through the use of certain theater games.[2]

Players who get lost in character, emotions, and attitudes and are concerned about "how am I doing?" are confined in their heads: fragmented, isolated, lonely, nowhere to be found; they live in memory (not in the present). Even the most skillful performance done in this

□ *Do not consider present time as clock time but rather as a timeless moment when all are mutually engaged in experiencing and experience, the outcome of which is as yet unknown.*

□ *The act of making the basket or the home run keeps player and spectator alike in a state of process, of becoming united in as-yet-undiscovered probabilities. Actors must be transformed into players.*

□ *At the first rehearsal period, director, players, and playwright may be meeting one another for the first time. It is necessary first to bring the players together within themselves, then together with their fellow players and with the words of the playwright into the playing area.*

□ *"How am I doing?" reflects the obsessive approval/disapproval syndrome.*

□ *The ball player must be detached (for the sake of greater involvement) at the moment he waits for the moving ball. He must become a spectator to the outcome. The same is true of theater game players.*

[1]See TOUCH AND BE TOUCHED, p. 104, and SPACE WALKS, pp. 101-3. As the final step in building trust, see Special Run-Through, p. 79.

[2]VOWELS AND CONSONANTS, p. 25, etc.

manner is empty and leaves all of us isolated one from the other. Audience and players alike are cheated.

All in the same playing space must be in waiting while the unfolding of the drama takes place. Not *waiting for*, but *in waiting*. To wait for is past/future. To stand in waiting is allowing the unknown — the new, the unexpected, perhaps the art (life) moment to approach.

The Director

Theater games are directors' techniques. Each game, almost without exception, was developed for the sole purpose of getting something to happen on stage. They resolve problems in blocking, character, emotion, timing, the players' relations with the audience. Each and every theater game is a magic wand, and as such taps the intuitive, producing a transformation not only in the actor/player, but in the director/sidecoach as well.

A need to create peerage while at the same time being certain of the director's touch upon the production necessitates a nonauthoritarian approach. During play, all meet in present time, involved with one another, off the subject,[1] and ready for free connecting, communicating, responding, experiencing, experimenting, and flowing through to new horizons of the self. Direction comes not from the outside, but from the players' needs and the theatrical needs of the moment.

There are variations of skill, talent, and genius in each group that plays. But at no matter what level, whether community playhouse or professional theater, an interesting performance is within the capacity of any group.

If you are concerned with process, stay away from theater clichés that have become labels. The avoidance of labels frees thought, for it allows the player to share in a unique way. Actors develop a sensitivity to the problem of relation to the audience. Imposing a label before its organic meaning is fully understood prevents this direct experiencing, aborting intuitive response.

In some cases, the cast will contain actors with previous theater experience who will initially use the conventional stage terminology and may even be an-

☐ *Intuition emerges in the right half of the brain, in the metaphoric mind, the X-area, the area of knowledge which is beyond the restrictions of culture, race, education, psychology, and age; it is deeper than the survival dress of mannerisms, prejudices, intellectualism, and borrowings most of us wear to live out our daily lives.*

☐ *Authoritarians believe they know the only way.*

☐ *Substitute* **Share with your audience! You're rocking the boat! Share your voice!** *for such terms as "blocking" and "projection."*

☐ *Recognition of* **Share with your audience!** *becomes the responsibility of each individual player and produces a more spontaneous movement than any comment on good or bad blocking.*

[1]See my *Theater Game File* (CEMREL, 1975), p. 4.

noyed with your non-use of it. However, this will gradually disappear as you slowly establish the theater game terminology. Theater game coaching phrases evoke discovery.[2]

Theater Techniques

Theater techniques are far from sacred. Styles in theater change radically with the passing of years. The actuality of the communication is far more important than the method used. Methods alter to meet the needs of time and place.

When a theater technique or stage convention has become a ritual and the reason for its inclusion in the list of actors' skills is lost, it is useless. An artificial barrier is set up when techniques are separated from direct experiencing. No one separates batting a ball from the game itself.

Techniques are not mechanical devices — a neat little bag of tricks, each neatly labeled, to be pulled out by the actor when necessary. For unless the actor is unusually intuitive, such rigidity in teaching, which neglects inner development, is invariably reflected in performance.

When an actor knows "in the bones" there are many ways to do and say one thing, techniques will come (as they must) from the total self.

☐ *The techniques of the theater are the techniques of communicating.*

☐ *When the form of an art becomes static, and isolated techniques which make up the form are taught and adhered to strictly, growth of both individual and form suffer.*

☐ *It is by direct, dynamic awareness of an acting experience that experiencing and techniques are spontaneously wedded, freeing the actor for the flowing, endless pattern of stage behavior. Spolin theater games do this.*

[2]Look over the Glossary of Sidecoaching Phrases, pp. 113-15.

Choosing the Play

It is difficult to set down a blueprint for choosing a play. However, there are a few specific questions which the director should address before making a final decision:

1. Who will my audience be?
2. How skillful are my actors?
3. Do I have a technical staff that can handle the effects the play will need?
4. Is it a play *I* can handle?
5. Is this merely a costumed lecture (moralizing)?
6. Will the play respond to my work on it?
7. Is the play worth doing?
8. Is the play theatrical?
9. Will it be a creative experience for all?
10. Will it be fun to do? Will it play?
11. Is it psychodrama?
12. Is it in good taste?
13. Will it give a fresh experience, provoke individual thought and thereby insight for the audience?
14. Are the parts (beats and/or scenes) within the play constructed so they can be brought to life?

Throughout rehearsal periods, constantly question:

1. How can the playwright's intent be clarified?
2. Are individual mannerisms getting in the way?
3. Should the scene be heightened visually with more purposeful blocking and business, unusual props or effects?
4. Are crowd or party scenes handled ineffectively? See Stage Picture, p. 39.
5. Should we play more?

The Director's Objective

If the intent of a theater game is understood by the director when presenting it to the players, a noticeable vitality and a high level of response in playing will emerge.

□ *Theater games hold within them the prefiguring of their solution in terms of stage conventions and behavior.*

As director, your concentration is on the script and what to use to bring it to life. Out of the very playing then, the life of the play itself will emerge for the director to see. Working this way sustains group agreement, the finding of solutions to stage problems through group playing.

Long before casting, you will have read the play through many times and will have sensed the playwright's intention and will have envisioned the play personally. To begin with, your "dream" play and the productions you remember must be discarded. Since a production is nourished by the skills, creativity, and energies of many, it is necessary for the director to realize that players and technicians cannot be pushed into preconceived patterns if live performances are hoped for. There are no solo flights!

☐ *Become very familiar with the games, so that you will know which games to give the players. This is essential for a harmonious, textured performance.*

Focus

"The [Spolin theater games] are artifices against artificiality, structures designed to almost fool spontaneity into being — or perhaps a frame carefully built to keep out interferences in which the player waits. Important in the game is the 'ball' — the Focus, a technical problem, sometimes a double technical problem which keeps the mind (a censoring device) so busy rubbing its stomach and its head in opposite directions, so to speak, that genius (spontaneity), unguarded 'happens'."

— *Film Quarterly*

☐ *Full-body attention to focus transforms actors into players.*

The director helps actors find and keep the focus which sets the game in motion, and all become fellow players as they attend to the same problem from different points of view. Thus, with the focus between all, dignity and privacy are maintained and true peerage can evolve. Trust the focus! Let it work for you.

The effort to stay on focus and the uncertainty about outcome diminish obstructing attitudes, create mutual support, and generate organic involvement in the playing as it unfolds, as all, director (sidecoach) and actors (players), are tripped into the present moment, alerted to solve the problem. An eight-year-old player very aptly once said, "It takes all your strength to stay on focus."

Keep your eye on the ball!

☐ *Theater games give the player a task to perform; the director selects the game that will solve the performance and playing problem.*

Casting

In casting, infinite insight is required of the director, who is looking, after all, not for a finished piece of work but for a tone of voice, a presence, a bodily quality — an indefinable "something" which initially is only sensed. (The amount of work that it will take to develop each person fully must be considered.) An actor may have the character qualities that are wanted but have so little background or so many set patterns and mannerisms that it may not be possible to achieve what is needed in the limited rehearsal period.

A method of casting that can be done quite successfully with new people is a combination of the try-out and improvisation. This tends to relax the actors, and, in a tension-free atmosphere, the director is more likely to see everyone's possibilities clearly. Give those trying out a quick verbal resumé of the scene; the Where (the set) and the Who (the characters). Or give a scene around a problem which is similar to, but not the same as, the play. After the game has been played (ad-libbed), the actors can read for the play.

In some cases, the director reads the full play to the assembled group prior to casting. If this is done, the director should take care to read with as little characterization as possible, to avoid subsequent imitation by the actors. Sometimes scenes are read. Or, actors are simply given "sides"[1] to read with little if any comment by the director.

Whatever procedure is chosen, it is best that the director's anxieties be well concealed. Casting is a tense period for one upon whose choice so much depends. You must be certain that the seed of the character exists within each one who is finally cast.

☐ *Another casting method, if the group has been together for a long time, is to do a run-through in* GIBBERISH *(see p. 53).*

[1]See p. 14 on sides.

Evaluation

For all our attempts to clear the atmosphere of authoritarian vocabulary, we may not always succeed. During rehearsals when so much is at stake, the director's word becomes very important. When evaluating, speak in terms of what was or was not being done on stage.

Workshops, in which each game has a focus and usually an evaluating audience, will help. In this kind of evaluating environment everyone strives to be free of subjective critiquing. Good/bad notes change to **On focus!**, **Off focus!** Did they solve the problem?

By transcending critiquing (a personal opinion) and evaluating on the basis of what works or does not work, you will find your new role as a guide and be able to lead the group to the performance, for *the needs of the theater are the real master.*

□ *In any culture the controlling relationship of parent/teacher to child/student is very ingrained.*

□ *Avoid approval/disapproval. Avoid good/bad.*

The Director as Sidecoach

The director's energies must at all times be focused on finding, for both the actors and technical crews, deeper insights and perspectives to enhance the final theater communication.

Fortunate indeed is the director who begins with highly gifted actors and experienced technicians. The work will thus be more easily implemented. However, from the first choice of the play to the discovery of the lighting plot, what is finally selected is the result of the sensitivity, awareness, and good taste of the director — the catalytic agent, seeking to channel the energies of many diverse people into one unified action.

□ *The director is the eye and ear of the audience to come.*

□ *The director during workshops and rehearsals transforms into a fellow player.*

Sidecoaching

Sidecoaching and the special sidecoaching vocabulary of Spolin Theater Games attempt to do away with all authoritarian directives and the accompanying approval/disapproval syndrome, and to allow time and space for movement, interaction, and transformation.

Sidecoaching is one of the generating facets (energizers) of the theater game process.

Sidecoaching will support you, together with your players who are getting the message. Sidecoaching reaches the total organism. The sidecoaching phrases arise spontaneously out of what is emerging on stage and are given at the time players are in movement. This is a method of keeping the player and director in contact.

Sidecoaching must guide players toward and into energy exchange, keeping the play *flowing* around all players, thus creating interaction, movement, and transformation.

Sidecoaching alerts the director to the necessity of producing and/or maintaining rising energy. Out of this energy release, character, emotion, and relationships are formed into the shape of the desired performance.

Sidecoaching directives must be free of authoritarian control, non-directional; they are evocative, resourceful, intimate whisperings; urgings; potentiators; stimulating, provoking, coaxing catalysts.

To sidecoach effectively, use a simple, direct calling out: *Share the stage picture! See the buttons on John's coat! Share your voice with the audience! Contact! See it with your feet! No playwriting! Help your fellow player who isn't playing!*

Such comments are worth a dozen lectures on blocking, projection, giving visibility to space objects, etc. When they are given as part of the process, the actor effortlessly moves out of a huddled position, gives the table its space, and sees fellow players.

The player who looks out inquiringly when first hearing your sidecoaching need only be coached *Hear my voice! Give it no attention!* or *Listen to my voice but keep right on going!*

Do not confuse players with a barrage of pointless sidecoaching. Wait for the emerging play. Remember, you

☐ *Sidecoaching brings you on stage with your fellow players, who are also swimming upstream toward performance. By allowing yourself to enter the role of sidecoach you and your players become part of the growth process simultaneously.*

☐ *Find the off-balance moment.*

☐ *Great care must be taken to see that the coaching does not disintegrate into an approval/disapproval involvement — a command to be obeyed!*

☐ *An authoritarian is one in charge — parent, teacher, boss, director, dictator. By demanding that things be done his or her way, he or she manipulates, blocking off the intuitive.*

☐ *Whether giving or taking as sidecoach, every individual must find his or her own way through personal effort.*

☐ *Your coaching voice reaches the total inner/outer self without stopping the playing, and the player moves accordingly.*

too are a player.

This book contains a glossary of sidecoaching phrases, pp. 113-15, for your use. Each theater game in the book also includes suggested sidecoaching. Sidecoaching appears in large, bold italics in the right-hand, narrow, columns. It is followed by evaluation questions on the game in lighter italics.

Spontaneity — The Off-Balance Moment

Can spontaneity be achieved with a written script and more or less prescribed stage movements? With repeated performances?

Discussion with your cast on this matter does not really address the problem. Discussion is cut off — in the head. Breaking up old set patterns is what is required. How to coax and stimulate the intuition to evoke the genii resting in all of us? Stop to play a theater game. Give appropriate sidecoaching during rehearsals. Hold workshops regularly during the run of your show.

□ *Fear of spontaneity is common. There is safety in old familiar feelings and actions. Spontaneity asks that we enter an unknown territory — ourselves!*

□ *Some players experiencing a moment or two of true spontaneity become uncomfortable and frightened. This off-balance moment is the gateway. Support and applaud this glimpse for everyone of sensing unrealized possibilities.*

The Director's Ability to Inspire

People who are inspired may pace the floor or talk animatedly. Eyes sparkle, ideas pour forth, and the body releases its holds. If many people are inspired simultaneously, then the very air around them seems to sparkle and dance with excitement.

Inspiration in the theater comes out as energy. This does not mean leaping wildly about the stage (although this might help at times). It is the intensity of the director's focus on what the players are doing, plus the use of skillful sidecoaching, which subsequently prods the actors into extending themselves, into reaching beyond. Sometimes the director must literally *pour* this energy into the cast as one might pour water into a glass, and in most instances, the cast will respond and be able to pour it right back again.

□ *Inspiration can be described as reaching beyond one's self or as reaching deeper into one's self.*

□ *An actor once commented, "Playing to you is like playing to a full house at the opera!" This is the kind of energy a director must give to actors.*

Never for one moment should you show tiredness or boredom, for the director without energy does more harm to the play than can be imagined. If this tiredness should occur, it is far better to stop rehearsals completely and have the stage manager take over for a sit-down line rehearsal.

Any actor (player) without energy is worthless, being out of contact with the ongoing activity. The same holds true for the director, who must not make "inspiring the actors" a mere phrase. Indeed, when a lag in rehearsals does occur, one would do well to look to oneself. Ask yourself:

□ *Play a traditional game rather than continue with a lifeless rehearsal.*

1. Am I giving enough energy?
2. Am I staying overlong on mechanics?
3. Which players need individual attention?
4. Do they need more workshops?
5. Are rehearsals too drawn out?
6. Am I nagging the players?
7. Am I attacking them?
8. Are the actors working at odds with me?
9. Is the problem physical or psychological?
10. Am I just being a traffic manager?
11. Is it necessary to stimulate more spontaneity?
12. Am I using the actors as puppets?
13. Am I overanxious?
14. Am I asking them for more than they can give me at this time?
15. Am I reaching the intuitive?

If you search for and face each problem directly (honestly), your own ingenuity, spontaneity, and energy can provide the inspiration to your players.

Rehearsals

The overall rehearsal schedule can be broken down into three periods. The first period (see p. 22) is for warming up the director and the players, for laying the groundwork in relationships and attitudes to the play and to each other. The second period (see p. 42) is the spontaneous, creative one, the digging sessions, where all energies are channeled toward full artistic potential in realizing the text. The third period (see p. 69) is for polishing and integrating all production facets into a unity.

□ *If the rehearsal period is one of tensions, anxieties, competitiveness, and bad tempers, this will be absorbed by the actors along with their parts and will hover like a shadow over the finished work.*

The amount of time spent in rehearsal depends upon the actors' availability. Professionals, of course, have no other commitments. But with community theater groups, the opposite is true, and the amount of free time is limited.

Plan the rehearsal schedule so that every player is working at every possible moment. It is advisable to think in terms of two kinds of time: clock-time and energy-time. Energy-time is the more valuable, for the director can get as much from actors in two hours of inspired, excited rehearsal as in six hours of boredom and fatigue.

Whether it is a vignette, a one-act play, or a three-act play — whether the clock-time is eight hours or sixty — the rehearsal time can be calculated by noting what must be covered in each session. If the group meets only three times a week and each session can have only a maximum of two hours, the director must schedule rehearsals accordingly. When the time arrives for costume parades, dress rehearsal, etc., extra hours will of course have to found for these time-consuming activities.

☐ *If the atmosphere is relaxed, social, and joyous with the excitement of the work at hand and the anticipation of the show to come, this too will be evident in the final production. When actors are enjoying their roles, then the audience will be relaxed and an extra note of pleasure is added to their viewing.*

Theme

Theme is the moving thread that weaves itself into every beat of the play or scene. It intertwines and shows itself within the simplest gesture of the player and in the last bits of trim on the costume.

In simple terms the director should think of theme as the thread that links all the separate parts together — a means for keeping costume, set design, play, technicians, director, and actors together, working under one banner.

Sometimes, watching and listening, it is a single word or phrase that sparks us; sometimes it is simply a nonverbal feeling that develops. The director may find the theme before rehearsals begin, or may be well into rehearsal before it appears. In some cases it never shows itself. The director must be careful, however, not to be rigid about finding a theme and in desperation impose one upon the play, producing a dead end rather than an open path for all. Randomness could be a theme.

☐ *The circus theme for "The Clown Who Ran Away" surfaced after a few rehearsals. Bobby Kay, a clown from the Clyde Beatty Circus, was brought in to tell the cast about clowns and clown makeup. He so entranced the cast with his stories of the traditions behind clown performances and the dignity with which each clown puts his mark upon his face that when the time came for actors to create their own clown characters, not one made just a "funny face." Each struggled to place the mark upon the face with all the individuality of a real clown creating a personal characterization.*

The Acting "Side"

Now the play is cast and ready for rehearsals. What about scripts? Some directors use full scripts (book); others use "sides," which consist of one or two words of the cue and the subsequent full speech of the individual actor. The side can be creatively stimulating, strengthens timing, and is to be preferred.

It should be typed on 8½ x 11 paper and folded horizontally so that it may be held easily. The addition of the action cue along with the word cue will eliminate much of the problem of slow pickups. The action cue is the word or combination of words which sets the next actor in motion.

If "action cue" is not clear to the actors, an explanation should be given at the time the sides are introduced: Do we begin to answer another person while he is still speaking, or do we start thinking about our answer after he has finished? "While he is speaking."

Carry on a conversation with the actors to point up the problem: Do we always wait until the other person has stopped speaking (action—the actors are already answering) or do we sometimes break into their conversation? Some have already broken into the above speech and have answered, "We don't always wait."

Point out how they were able to anticipate the outcome of the discussion. Suggest observing people as they converse to determine which are the action cues and which are the word cues. Sometimes, of course, both cues will be identical (as in a cry for help).

The acting side prevents an actor from reading the others' lines subvocally and eliminates any mouthing. The actor must *listen* and *watch* fellow players in order to follow the action and know when to come in. Unable to memorize the others' lines, the actor is forced to act upon the spoken word.

Only stage directions which lead to action or dialogue (entrances, exits, etc.) should be included on the sides. It is best to avoid many of the playwright's directions (such as "speaks happily," "heaves a heart-rending sigh," or "winks knowingly"). Let the physical actions and facial expressions come from the actors' own inner action and from the dialogue itself. There will be plenty of op-

□ *A "side":*
Cue: quiet.................hear me!
Line: All right, if you feel that way.
Cue: Get out ....Get out!
Line: I will, and don't expect me back!
(Exit)
In the first cue and speech, "quiet" is the action cue, and "hear me" (coming some words later) is the word cue. In the second cue and speech, the first "get out" is the action cue, and the second is the word cue. The inner action (bodily response) begins at the action cue; and the actor is ready for action and response upon hearing the word cue.

portunity in the second rehearsal period, when actors are free of all restrictions, for you to bring in the playwright's stage directions to further the action.

Chapter 2:
WORKSHOPS

Whether workshops precede, follow, are interspersed during a rehearsal, or are held on separate days is the director's decision. What games to use depends on what takes place during rehearsal. For instance, when it is obvious that actors are reading lines and ignoring the very person they are speaking to, you have a wide choice of theater games to play: SPACE WALKS, pp. 101-3, TOUCH AND BE TOUCHED/SEE AND BE SEEN, p. 104, and GIBBERISH: SELLING, p. 53, to name a few.

The following suggested workshop is recommended before or just after the first sit-down rehearsal. It may take up one or two sessions:

EXPOSURE/TUG OF WAR
PLAY BALL
THREE CHANGES
MIRROR
WHO IS THE MIRROR?
FOLLOW THE FOLLOWER[1]

The selection of theater games to be played in later workshops will be up to the director.

□ *Theater games do not displace rehearsals. Pursuing the script and playing go hand in hand to achieve harmony in performance.*

[1] FEELING SELF WITH SELF, p. 24, and WHO STARTED THE MOTION?, p. 28, are also good warm-up games.

Seeing and Not Staring

An actor must not only look, but must *see*. Staring is a curtain in front of the eyes as surely as when the eyes are closed. It is isolation.

Staring is easily detected by watching for certain physical characteristics: a flat look to the eyes and a rigidity to the body. GIBBERISH will quickly show you the degree to which this exists.

When the actor *sees* even momentarily, observe how the face and body become more pliant and more natural as muscle tension and fear of contact disappear. When one player sees another, direct contact *without attitudes* is the result. Recognition of a fellow player gives one a glimpse of oneself.

□ *Actors who stare but do not see prevent themselves from directly experiencing their environment and from entering into relation with the onstage world.*

EXPOSURE

Purpose: To keep players alert, working in the present.

Focus: None for Part 1. In Part 2, on doing something specified by the director.

Description: Full group counts off into two teams. Team 1 stands in a single line facing the seated audience (Team 2).

Part 1: Team 1 is to stand and do nothing.

Part 2: When players on Team 1 show signs of discomfort, director gives players a task to accomplish, such as counting the floorboards or chairs in the room. Players are coached to keep counting until signs of discomfort are gone and players show bodily relaxation and release. When signs of discomfort are gone, reverse teams.

Notes: 1. The purpose is to keep the players standing *unfocused*. Stay with Part 1 until all standing players are visibly uncomfortable. Some players will giggle and shift from foot to foot; others will freeze in position or try to appear nonchalant.

2. If audience team members start to laugh, ignore the laughter and emphasize the sidecoaching directive, *We'll look at you!*

3. No evaluation until both teams have played both parts.

4. Allow each player the personal experience of discovering organically the power of *focus*, of something-to-do. "The bodily discomfort went away." Why? "I had something to do."

Part 1: *Do nothing!*
We'll look at you! That's all!
(Do not call individual players by name; coach to all players):
You do nothing! We'll watch!

Part 2: *Count all the chairs in the room!*
You are doing the most important thing of your life!
Keep counting! Start over again!

How did you feel when you were first standing in front of us?
(Guide away from description of emotions. "I felt self-conscious." Ask: "I don't know what you mean by self-conscious. How did your stomach feel? Your neck?")
Audience, how did players look when they were standing doing nothing?

TUG OF WAR

Purpose: To awaken the invisible communication among players.

Focus: On keeping the space rope as a connecting link between players.

Description: One team at a time, each player tries to pull the other over a center line, exactly as in playground tug of war. Here, however, the rope is not visible but made of space substance. Ask players to *Pick a partner of equal strength!* This message to the individual psyche is received with laughter. It creates mutuality — a bond — contest not competition. As each team plays the others observe.

Notes: 1. Read notes on SPACE SUBSTANCE, p. 68.
2. Play the space rope and space ball games with your group until the phenomenon of objects in space, not in the head, has been experienced by everyone and is understood by your group.
3. As your group becomes facile with this game played in pairs, add more and more players to both ends of the rope.

Keep the rope in space! And out of the head!
Keep the rope between you!
Use your full bodies to pull! Your back! Your feet!
Stay on the same rope!
Pull! Pull! Pull!

Audience players, were the players on the same rope?
Did the rope connect players?
Was the rope in space or in the players' heads? Players, was the rope in space or in your heads?
Do players agree with audience?
Does audience agree with players?

THREE CHANGES

Purpose: To improve players' powers of observing.

Focus: On other player to see where changes were made.

Description: Full group counts off into teams of two players each. All teams play simultaneously. Partners observe one another, noting dress, hair, accessories, and so on. Partners then turn backs on each other and each makes three changes in personal appearance: they part hair, untie a shoelace, switch watch to the other arm, etc. When ready, partners again face each other and each tries to identify what changes the other has made.

Notes: 1. By changing partners and asking for four changes, this game can be played with excitement for some time.
2. Change partners again and ask for five, six, seven, and even eight changes, observing the back for changes as well.
3. This leads right into MIRROR, p. 20.

PLAY BALL

Purpose: To focus players' attention on a moving space object.

Focus: On keeping the ball in space and out of the head.

Description: Players count off into two large teams. One team is the audience. Then switch. Working individually within the team, players each start to toss a ball against a wall, etc. The balls are all imaginary, made of a space substance. When the players are all in motion, the director will change the speed at which balls are moving.

Notes: 1. Read notes on SPACE SUBSTANCE, p. 68.

2. The player knows when the ball is in the space or in the head. When it is in the space it will "appear" to player and audience alike.

3. The question to audience players, "Was the ball in space or in your heads?" is important in that it acknowledges the audience's responsibility to observe the emergence if it should occur. The audience is as responsible for keeping focus as is the playing team.

4. After evaluation of the first team, have the next team play. Did the second team benefit from evaluation of the first team?

5. Emphasize use of full body to keep the ball in motion. Players should leave the game with all physical effects of having played an active game of catch.

6. Words used by the director in the presentation of this game must be carefully chosen. Players are not asked to pretend, to imagine, to make the ball real. Players are simply sidecoached to keep the ball in space and out of the head.

Variations: 1. Play same game with a space-substance ball that changes weight. As ball becomes lighter and heavier, players' bodies may seem to become lighter and heavier or to move in slow motion. Do not bring this point to players' attention during play.

2. Play other games — dodge ball, volleyball, baseball with space-substance ball.

The ball is moving in verrrryyy slowww motion!
Catch the ball in very slow motion!
Now the ball is moving normally!
Use your full body to throw the ball!
Keep your eye on the ball!
Change! Speed it up!
Throw and catch the ball as fast as you can!
Back and forth as fast as you can!
Normal once more!
Allow the ball its time in space!

Players, was the ball in the space or in your heads?
Audience, do you agree with players?
Was the ball in your heads or in the space?
Players, did you allow the ball its time in space? Audience, do you agree?

Var. #1: *The ball is becoming lighter!*
It is one hundred times lighter!
Now it is becoming heavy!
Use your whole body to throw the ball!
Keep your eyes on the ball!

——MIRROR——————————————————————————

Purpose: To help players see with the full body; to reflect, not imitate, the other.

Focus: On exact mirror reflection of the initiator's movements.

Description: Players count off into teams of two players. One player becomes A, the other B. All teams play simultaneously. A faces B. A reflects all movements initiated by B, head to foot, including facial expressions. After a time, positions are reversed so that B reflects A.

Notes: 1. Watch for assumptions, which prevent reflection. For example, if B makes a familiar movement, does A anticipate and assume the next move, or does A stay with B?
2. Watch for true reflection. If B uses right hand, does A use right hand or opposite hand? Do not bring this aspect of the game to players' attention cerebrally. Playing WHO IS THE MIRROR? (following) will bring an organic understanding of reflection.
3. Changeover or reverse should be made without stopping the flow of movement between players.

B initiate!
A reflect!
Big full-body movements!
Reflect only what you see! Not what you think you see!
Keep the mirror between you!
Reflect fully — head to toe!
Change!
Now A initiate movement and B reflect!
Know when you initiate!
Know when you are reflecting!
Change! . . . Change! . . .

Is there a difference between reflection and imitation?
Did you know when you were initiating? Reflecting?

——WHO IS THE MIRROR?————————————————

Purpose: To prepare for FOLLOW THE FOLLOWER.

Focus: On concealing from audience which player is the mirror.

Description: Teams of two. Before "calling curtain," players decide which player will be the initiator and which the mirror. This game is played exactly as in MIRROR, except that the director does not call out **Change!** One player initiates all movement, the other reflects, and both players attempt to conceal which one is the mirror from the audience players. When the two players are moving, the director calls out the name of one player. Audience players raise hands if that player appears to be the mirror. Director then calls out the name of the other player for audience hands. Both players continue playing during the voting without stopping, until the vote is unanimous for one or the other player or until stalemate is reached.

(To audience):
Which player is the mirror?

—FOLLOW THE FOLLOWER——————————————

Purpose: To bring about a flowing movement and change, through reflection.

Focus: On following the follower.

Description: Teams of two. One player becomes the mirror, the other the initiator. Director will start the players playing MIRROR, calling **Change!** at intervals for players to reverse positions. When players are initiating and reflecting with large body movements, call **On your own!** Players then reflect each other without initiating.

Notes: 1. Start players on their own only when they are in full-body motion.

2. This is tricky — players are not to initiate but are to follow the initiator. Both are at once the initiator and the mirror. Players reflect themselves being reflected.

3. Following the follower quiets the mind and frees players to enter a time, a space, a moment with no room for attitudes, thinking, or inquiry. Players recognize that they are intertwined with one another in a nonphysical, nonverbal, nonpsychological, nonanalytical, nonjudgmental area of their free inner selves.

Reflect!
Know when you initiate!
Reflect only what you see—not what you think you see!
Change!

(Director may enter the playing area to check player initiations.)

Heighten full-body movements!
You are on your own!
Follow the follower!
Keep the mirror between you!
Follow the follower!

(During actual play; to a moving player):
Did you initiate that movement?
Or did you reflect what you saw?
Audience players, do you agree with this player?

Chapter 3:
THE FIRST REHEARSAL PERIOD

Suggestions

Great fear will sometimes arise in the early rehearsals that you have erred in your choice of actors. If this is really so, you must recast quickly, for your attitude will affect everyone.

Without telling the cast, select two players for barometers: one whose response is high and one whose response is low. This way you will always know if you are giving too much or too little in rehearsals.

A few more suggestions:

1. Do not allow actors to keep their eyes glued to scripts when others are reading. Watch for this even at sit-down readings. Use UNRELATED CONVERSATIONS, p. 96, to remind the actors to see and to listen to others.
2. Avoid artificial reading habits from the first moment. Play GIBBERISH, p. 53, to counteract artificiality.
3. Make cue pick-ups natural by having the players work on action cues. *Do not handle this mechanically.* If it becomes necessary to work on word cues, wait until the latter part of the second or early part of the third rehearsal period.
4. Avoid setting character, lines, business, or blocking too early. A "rough-in" is all that is needed.
5. Details are unimportant in the first period. Once the characters and the relationships are set, it will be simple to bring in details. The life of each scene within the play must be found first.

☐ *You must trust your casting.*

☐ *Premature setting kills the fragile emerging intuition.*

☐ *Do not nag the players.*

The First Reading

As a warm-up to the first sit-down reading, play the game FEELING SELF WITH SELF, p. 24.

Then, using sides or scripts, sit with the actors in a circle or in a close group within which all can see one another. Have the cast read the first act, stopping for pronunciation problems, typographical errors, and (if the script is new) changes.

Following this, play VOWELS AND CONSONANTS and SPELLING, pp. 25-26. After SPELLING read a few scenes from the script, spelling the words as you go. Follow this with SLOW MOTION and SINGING DIALOGUE, p. 26. Continue to present this series until actors are free of the words, which have been cleansed of personal meaning, and are addressing one another. This may take as little as one hour as many as three or more sessions.

After two or three sit-down readings using the above games, the group should be relaxed, familiar with the script and each other, and in a pleasant anticipatory mood. When individuals realize that learning the lines, interpreting the script, forming the characters, etc., are *not* required at this time, a great sense of release will be evident. Everyone enters the spirit of playing, freed of tensions.[1]

The growth process has begun. Remember, all grow at different rates! How far players have come from the starting point is the measure of individual growth.

□ *First reading:*
1. *Director reads script (optional).*
2. *Parts are given out.*
3. *All read their lines aloud. Clean up pronunciation and typographical errors on sides. Don't be afraid to sidecoach during reading.*
4. VOWELS AND CONSONANTS, p. 25.
5. SPELLING, p. 26.
6. SLOW MOTION, p. 26.
7. SINGING DIALOGUE, p. 26.
8. *Second read-through, without stopping.*

□ *Is your anxiety showing?*

---

[1]Other excellent games to use at this time are UNRELATED CONVERSATIONS, p. 96, and EXTENDED SOUND, p. 67.

—Feeling Self with Self—

Purpose: Full-body perception of self.

Focus: On feeling self with the body part that is side-coached.

Description: Players sit quietly and respond.

Notes: 1. Feeling Self with Self can be used alone or with Space Walks, pp. 101-3.

2. Coach, *Keep your eyes open!* if necessary. This exercise should bring players and director into the room. Closed eyes can be a withdrawal into the head.

3. This game heightens awareness of the player's physical body. *Out of the head!*

4. It brings players into their own bodies (themselves) and into the playing space.

5. This game is excellent as a bridge from street to rehearsal hall.

Feel your feet in your stockings!
Feel your stockings on your feet!
Feel your feet in your shoes!
Feel your stockings on your legs!
Feel your legs in your stockings!
Feel your slacks or skirt over your legs!
Feel your legs in your slacks!
Feel your underclothing next to your body!
Feel your body in your underclothing!
Feel your blouse or shirt against your chest and your chest inside your blouse or shirt!
Feel your ring on your finger!
Feel your finger in your ring!
Feel the hair on your head and your eyebrows on your forehead!
Feel your tongue in your mouth!
Feel your ears!
Go inside and try to feel the inside of your head with your head!
Feel all the space around you!
Now let the space feel you!

Was there any difference between feeling your ring on your finger and feeling your finger in the ring?

——Vowels and Consonants——

Purpose: To become acquainted with the physiological structure of language; a respite from subjective thought or interpretation.

Focus: On contacting the vowels or consonants in a word as it is spoken.

Description: Six or eight players stand in a circle or in two lines. Each player is to begin a quiet conversation with the player opposite (eight players means four simultaneous conversations). Players are to *focus* on either the vowels or consonants as sidecoached in the words they speak without putting emphasis on them or changing speech patterns. Keeping voices low, players are to move back away from each other as far as space permits, then forward again as sidecoached.

Notes: 1. Wait until players are physiologically attentive to partners before coaching them to move away from each other.

2. Players can actually lower their voices as they put distance between them; conversations can be held in a murmur from as far away as forty feet.

3. The sidecoaching phrase, *Close eyes!* opens players to the fact that they are not lip reading. The whole body from head to foot is involved with the spoken word.

4. Have players think of words as sound which they shape or design into word patterns.

Part 1: *Vowels!*
Contact, feel, touch the vowels!
Let the vowels touch you!
Consonants!
Talk normally!
See, feel, focus on the consonants!

Part 2: *Move back from each other!*
Vowels! . . . Consonants!
Speak more softly than before!
Move as far back as possible!

Part 3: *Move in closer!*
Speak more softly yet!
Vowels! . . . Consonants!
Close your eyes!
Speak as quietly as possible!
Move into original positions!

Did you have a sense of making physical contact with the word spoken?
Was communication maintained throughout?
Did meaning emerge in the space between vowels and consonants?

— SPELLING

Purpose: To keep words empty of meaning.

Focus: On communicating to another player.

Description: Whole group breaks into teams of two or three. They hold conversations, spelling their words.

Notes: 1. Continue as long as spirits are high and all conversing is fluent. The excitement of a connection with fellow players will appear.
2. After players are familiar with the game, choose a small section of a script to read spelling. If your group finds this difficult, do not spend a long time with it.

Spell sensually!
See the letters!
Physically see the words in your mouth!

How much of the conversation was understood by the listener?
Did the speller see the letters?

— SLOW MOTION

Purpose: To put everyone in the same place.

Focus: On being in slow motion while reading the script.

Description: Part 1: Read the script in slow motion.
Part 2: Focus on slow motion while reading the script with regular rhythms.

The space around you is in slooow moootion!
You are sitting in slow motion!
Talking slowly is not talking in slow motion!

Did you feel as though the whole room was in slow motion?
Did objects and fellow players become present?

— SINGING DIALOGUE

Purpose: To create a *flow* of sound between players, making players and audience all one.

Focus: On extending dialogue to fellow player through singing.

Description: Two or more players. The situation (Where, Who, and What) is agreed upon. All dialogue is to be sung. Singing must be addressed to the fellow player.

Notes: 1. Good singing voices are not necessary, as this is an exercise in the extension of sound.
2. Players who recite words dramatically *(recitativo)* should be continually coached to jump to melody.
3. Do not impose melodic structure upon the players. If it comes, it should come naturally.
4. Singing permits elongation of the word. Singing also permits repetition.
5. The flow of sounds is a bridge to the intuition.

Sing out your words!
Heighten it!
Sing with your whole body!

Did players explore all the areas into which singing dialogue could lead?
Players, do you agree?

Warm-Ups

Regular general warm-ups are always recommended before rehearsal. Warm-ups remove any outside distractions actors may have brought with them. Warm-ups warm up! They get blood circulating. Warm-ups at the end of a low-energy rehearsal, on the other hand, lift spirits; they help season your play and players. Warm-ups make all present to each other. They help actors overcome personal differences.

Play traditional games first, especially those requiring physical action such as EXPLOSION TAG, PUSSY WANTS A CORNER or WHO STARTED THE MOTION?, pp. 27-28. Go on then to SPACE WALKS, pp. 101-3, PLAY BALL, p. 19, and EXPOSURE, p. 17. (FEELING SELF WITH SELF, p. 24, is also a good warm-up game.)

□ *Warm-ups bring all players into the same working space.*

— EXPLOSION TAG

Purpose: To crack players' protective armor.

Focus: None for this traditional game.

Description: Establish a relatively small area. A 20-by-20 foot space is about right for fifteen players. Half the group plays and half becomes audience. A regular game of tag is played within boundaries. Leader calls out "Not it!" Last player to call out becomes "it." Players may not step outside boundaries. When energy levels are high, director will add another rule that when tagged, player must take a moment to "explode." There is no set way to "explode."

Notes: 1. This tag game is a natural warm-up and lead-in to SLOW MOTION, p. 26, and, although you may have restrictions of time or noise levels, even a minute of EXPLOSION TAG is quite useful.

2. Explosion is a spontaneous action at the moment of being tagged.

Stay within boundaries!
Remember the boundaries!
(When energy level is high):
When you are tagged, take time to explode!
While pursuing another player, keep exploding!
Explode in any way you wish!
Fall on the floor!
Yell!
Explode!

PUSSY WANTS A CORNER

Purpose: To produce crises (off-balance moments). Players must interact.

Focus: To avoid becoming — to stop being — "it."

Description: Full group stands around the perimeter of the playing space, except for one player (the pussy), who stands in the middle. The spot where each person stands is "a corner." Player who is "it" approaches another player and says "Pussy wants a corner!" The reply to this is "See my next door neighbor." Pussy continues this dialogue with fellow players in turn, while trying to jump into a corner vacated by other players, whose business it is to trade places without pussy pouncing upon a corner. The odd player out, in such a case, is "it."

WHO STARTED THE MOTION?

Purpose: To view others surreptitiously.

Focus: On trying to keep the center player from finding the leader who starts the motion.

Description: Players stand in a circle. One player is sent from the room while another player is selected to be the leader who starts the motion. The outside player is called back, stands in the center of the circle, and tries to discover the leader who is leading the other players through different motions (moving hands, tapping feet, nodding heads, etc.). Leader may change motions at any time, sometimes even when the center player is looking directly at the leader. When the center player discovers the leader, two other players are chosen to take their places.

(Only if leader does not change the motion often enough):
Leader, change your movement when you get a chance!
Watch for the change, other players, without giving the leader away!

Notes: 1. This traditional game is an excellent warm-up to the MIRROR games, pp. 20, 92, 94-95, for it requires careful viewing of fellow players.

2. Immediately after playing this game, you may have players count off into teams of two for THREE CHANGES, p. 18, which leads into the MIRROR games.

Walk-Through Rehearsal

Set doors, stairs, etc., keeping settings general. If you are working on a costume play, give some suggestions to actors about what they will be wearing, whether it be hoop skirt or stiff collar.

Sidecoach during walk-through when necessary: ***Share the stage picture! Share your voice! Vowels! Consonants! Slooow motion! Slooow motion is more than moving slowly! The space around you is in slooow motion! Let your sight move in slooow motion! Breathe in slow motion!***

Actors continue to read and move about during these sidecoaching remarks. As the cast is by now familiar with your calling out, this will not interfere but will enhance what is happening on stage. (See that all hold the script in one hand, leaving the other hand free for action. Gripping the script with two hands is holding on for dear life and reflects an old childhood fear.)

As rehearsals (plus workshops) continue, the actors together with the director begin discovering unexpected freedoms. Continuing sidecoaching allows everyone to go deeper within themselves, the script, and fellow players.

In effect the director, intuitively and with insight, sidecoaches. What is then evoked usually solves the problem, whether in terms of relation, character, or emotion. Sidecoaching keeps intact the integrity of director and actor, yet allows each to share the fresh experience and develops total action out of which the meaning of the playwright is revealed and often transcended.

□ *Out of the onstage problems that begin to emerge will come the theater games to be played in your next workshop. While it may be true that your selection of a game is based on the special needs of one or two actors, all will benefit.*

□ *Reaching in is reaching out.*

□ *What is called interpretation begins to emerge in this holistic approach to the play, out of the union (merging) of director, players, and playwright.*

Where (The Set)

Where are you?

It is essential for players to get inside the set (the playing field) and not just pass through it.[1]

The following example illustrates the use of the WHERE game. It comes from Bernard Downs, Professor of Oral Interpretation/Theatre, University of South Florida.

> Recently I was asked to coach a local community group of actors. They were touring the schools in a selection of scenes, including the first meeting of Katharina and Petruchio in *Taming of the Shrew* (II,i). Originally, their performances were over-controlled, neat, and dull. We commenced with the "Where Game" since they had not localized the scene, thinking of it as "only two people talking." By themselves they drew a floor plan, selecting the setting of a courtyard which included a fountain, bench, tree, bed of roses, rake and hoe. There were no physical props with the exception of a chair that was used for the bench. Their point of concentration (focus) was to use all the imaginary objects as they played the scene.
>
> Kate was gardening when Petruchio entered. As the scene progressed she tried to prevent his gaze by standing behind the tree, clipping branches as an excuse for this behavior. He pursued, picking up the branches. She went to the fountain, splashed him with water when he followed, and retrieved the hoe to protect herself. He grabbed the rake and started dueling, concluding with a peace offering of a rose. Sitting on the bench, she accepted it, gave it a brief whiff, and knocked him into the thorny bed of roses. For the first time, the physical world about them became vibrantly alive, and so were they.

Kate and Petruchio *played*. Like many of the games in this chapter, WHERE games are designed to make the physical world of the stage appear.

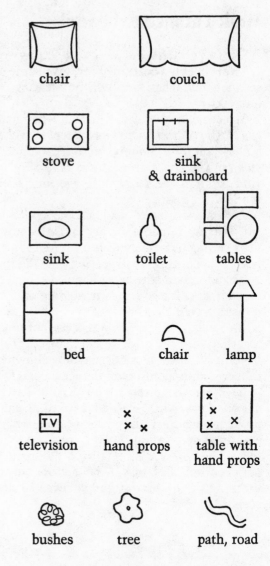

Suggested floorplan symbols

[1] See notes on Space Games, p. 100.

—WHERE GAME #1—

Purpose: To make the invisible visible.

Focus: On showing where you are by making physical contact with all the objects drawn on a floorplan. (The only physical objects actually needed on the stage will be chairs. The other objects are simply represented by chalk marks on a blackboard or a piece of paper and must be found in the stage space.) In other words, each player must in some way handle or touch everything drawn on the blackboard, sharing with the audience its visibility. To show Where, use a scene from the play.

Description: Two players. Each team of two is supplied with blackboard and chalk (or paper and pencils). They then agree on a place (Where) and plot out a floorplan. (If the team chooses a living room, they will plot out the sofa, chairs, coffee table, ashtrays, fireplace, etc.). Encourage each player to contribute a share of the items, using the standard floorplan symbols. (See illustrations, above.)

Notes: 1. The floorplan must face the stage where the on-stage players can see it.
2. The players are not to remember any of the items but refer to the floorplan as often as they wish during the exercise. This is a deliberate step to ease players from remembering (blanking the mind) and will give a great sense of relief if stressed. It is another step in helping the player relax the cerebral hold.
3. As much as possible, let the cast members discover variations for themselves.

Refer to the floorplan!
Out of your head — into the space!

Did players keep their focus?
Could objects have been used in a less pedestrian manner?
Are hands the only way of touching objects?
(Objects can be fallen against, leaned on, etc. Noses can be pressed against windows as easily as hands can open them.)

Did players share what they were doing with us?

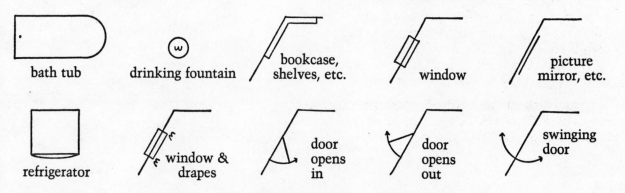

More suggested floorplan symbols

—WHERE GAME #2—————————————————

Purpose: To show players how a place can be defined by the people who occupy it and what they are doing.

Focus: On showing Where.

Description: Two teams. One player goes on stage and shows Where through physical use of the objects. The first player to whom it has been communicated assumes a Who, enters the Where, and develops a relationship (role) with the Where and the other player. Other players join them as related characters (Who) in the Where and the general activity (What).

Example: Player goes on stage and shows the audience rows and rows of bookshelves. A second player enters and stands behind counter. He begins stamping cards which he removes from the inside cover of books. Third player enters, pushes cart to shelves, and begins stacking books. Other players enter the library Where.

Note: Other settings for WHERE GAME #2: train station, supermarket, airport, hospital waiting room, street scene, beach, schoolroom, art gallery, restaurant.

Slow motion!
Keep focus on Where!
Relate to fellow players!

Stage set

WHERE GAME #3

Purpose: To test whether the actors have succeeded in physicalizing the setting, making the invisible visible.

Focus: On showing an audience Where, Who, and What through use of and/or contact with all objects in the Where.

Description: Count off for teams of two to four players. Each team agrees on Where, Who, and What and sketches a floorplan of Where on paper. As Where, Who, and What are played out, each player (referring to the floorplan) must make contact with every object in the floorplan. Players place actual chairs needed in the playing area, tack the floorplan up for easy referral and call curtain when ready.

Example: Where = kitchen, Who = family members, What = eating breakfast. Floorplan includes refrigerator, cupboards, table, sink, etc.

Notes: 1. Always check what audience saw against the actual floorplan.
2. Coach players to avoid planning how to use each object, as pre-planning takes all spontaneity out of the playing.
3. Several other games are useful in making space visible. See PLAY BALL, p. 19, and TUG OF WAR, p. 18. Other WHERE games may be useful in *early* stages of rehearsal before the set is built and ready to be used by the actors.

Share with the audience!
Show! Don't tell!
Each player must contact every object on the floorplan!
Refer to it if necessary!
Keep objects in space and out of your head!
Refer to your floorplan!

Did players use all objects on the floorplan?
Audience, what objects did players show us?
Players, check them off against the actual floorplan.
Did players show Where, Who, and What?
Or did they tell?
Were objects in space or in players' heads?
Players, did you walk through tables?
Did players integrate use of objects with Where, Who, and What?

Give and Take

GIVE AND TAKE games are very valuable early in rehearsals. They are exercises in hearing and listening.

Actors must *listen* to their fellow players and *hear* everything they say. An actor must *look* and *see* everything that is going on. This is the only way players can play together. If actors can see and hear a fellow player opposite them *through* the character being played, their work will be free of acting.

☐ *Actors who see another and listen rather than mouthing or subvocally reading the other's lines as memorized along with their own, will be relieved of posing.*

☐ GIVE AND TAKE *keeps the stage picture clean.*

—TAKE AND GIVE————————————————

Purpose: To intensify communication among players.

Focus: On taking.

Description: The full stage is alerted through sidecoaching when a player is taking. All others must *Give!* Often a player does not realize that he or she is taking. The simplest movement or sound is to take! Sidecoaching makes players aware.

Note: Used frequently during rehearsals, TAKE AND GIVE produces a full-stage flash of excitement for players and audience alike.

Gary is taking!
Susan is taking!
————— is taking!
Others give!

—GIVE AND TAKE WARM-UP————————

Purpose: To help players connect with one another.

Focus: On seeing and hearing.

Description: Players stand in a circle. Any player may start a movement. If any player is moving all other players must hold (no movement). Any player can make a motion at any time but must hold if another player starts a motion. Sounds may be considered movements.

Note: "Hold" is used instead of "freeze." "Freeze" is total stoppage; "hold" is waiting to move as soon as one can do so.

Hold your movement!
Take!
Continue the flow of your movement!
Hold when another player moves!
Take!
Give!

Los Angeles Public Library

Los Feliz Branch

4/26/2022   7:45:42 PM

- PATRON RECEIPT -
  - CHARGES -

Item Number: 37244113577655
Title: Improvisation for the theater : a handbook
Due Date: 5/17/2022

Item Number: 37244049302921
Title: Theater games for rehearsal : a director's
Due Date: 5/17/2022

To Renew: www.lapl.org or 888-577-5275

Big Read 2022: Thi Bui's
The Best We Could Do
lapl.org/big-read

--Please retain this slip as your receipt--

GIVE AND TAKE

Purpose: To be in a state of nonverbal agreement with partner, while in readiness to act with the other team.

Focus: On listening/hearing with partner to know when to give and take.

Description: (Two tables, each with two chairs, are useful for this exercise.) Players count off into teams of four. Teams subdivide into teams of two. Each subteam (sitting at its own table) pursues a separate conversation. While continuing separate conversations, both subteams must hear the other subteam so as to know when to give or take.

Part 1: Director calls **Table 1** and **Table 2** until how to play becomes clear to both subteams. Both subteams begin conversing at the same time. When Table 1 is called, Subteam 2 must fade out (submerge action) and give focus to Subteam 1. When Table 2 is called, Subteam 1 fades. Fade-out is not a freeze; players at table out of focus hold action, relationship, and conversation silently in no motion but stay prepared to continue actively when it is time to take focus once more.

Part 2: When mutual giving of focus to opposite subteam is understood, players are asked to continue their conversations, giving focus back and forth without being sidecoached.

Part 3: Continuing as above, both subteams try to *take* the focus from the other. The subteam which *holds* the attention of the audience has taken the focus.

Part 4: Both subteams give and take the focus without sidecoaching.

Notes: 1. Players on subteams learn to give and take as *one* unit. This develops receiving and sending abilities on a nonverbal level.

2. Use **Give and take!** as sidecoaching in any game whenever players all move and talk at the same time without hearing one another.

3. See TWO SCENES, pp. 160-63 in *Improvisation for the Theater*, for the original exercise.

Part 1: ***Table 1! Table 2 fade!***
Keep relationship within the fade!
Do not freeze!
Sit relaxed in no motion!
Table 2! Table 1 fade!

Part 2: ***Give! Play the game!***
Play as one unit!

Part 3: ***Take! Take!*** (Until focus is taken. Audience will know when focus is taken.)

Part 4: ***You are on your own!***
Give and take!
Know when to give!
Know when to take!
Play the game!

Subteam 1, did you have trouble knowing when your partner wanted to give?
Audience, could you tell when one member of a subteam didn't want to give and the other did?
Players, did you take the focus in Part 4 before the other team had given it?
Other subteam, do you agree?
Audience, do you agree?

—CONVERGE AND RE-DIVIDE—

Purpose: To help players become aware of focus.

Focus: On giving and taking the focus from fellow players.

Description: Teams of four, six, or eight players agree on Where, Who, and What, then divide into subteams of two players who are in an immediate relationship.

Example: Where = a party; Who = guests; What = eating, drinking, etc. During playing, subteams give and take focus from each other as in GIVE AND TAKE. At intervals, director calls *Converge!* and all players come together and find a common action, for instance, getting food at a buffet table. When the director calls *Re-divide!*, subteams must split, and the players continue with new partners, again using the give and take technique. The director calls *Converge!* and *Re-divide!* until players end in their original subteam relationships.

Notes: 1. When *Converge!* is called out, full group of players in interaction results. It is then that the new pairing-off occurs.

2. To quicken understanding, it is recommended that all teams go through the example of Where, Who, and What given above. All players simply converge at a refreshment table set up in the Where and re-divide into the room. Have all teams use the same Where.

3. When players do not give and take, two scenes are occurring simultaneously. When this happens during rehearsals, sidecoach *Two scenes!* to bring awareness to players.

4. Also see MIRROR Games and FOLLOW THE FOLLOWER, pp. 20-21, 92, 94-95.

Give and take!
When one team takes, other teams give!
Converge!
All teams converge!
Re-divide! New subteams!
Give and take!
Converge!

If Subteam A had the focus, did B and C use interesting ways of fading out?
Did players integrate converging and re-dividing with the overall event or scene?
Did players give and take for the enrichment of the event or scene?

Stage Movement (Blocking)

Blocking is essentially the choreography of stage movement. As simple as that may sound, moving actors about during a play may often be quite hazardous. You alone do not determine exactly where actors stand or how they get on or off the stage.

Blocking should facilitate movement, emphasize and heighten thought and action, strengthen relationships and underline conflicts. Blocking is the integration of the stage picture, a moving composition.

As long as the actor is constantly directed in the mechanics of stage movement and does not understand that stage movement can only grow out of involvement and interrelating, the actor can at best only remember the conventions and will therefore be unable to move naturally.

To test this theory, the following experiment was carried out by actors with little or no theater experience and only minimal workshop training. They were given two different scenes.

For the first scene, actors were given full scripts which contained the lines for all the characters plus the stage business and blocking as set down by the playwright. During the first rehearsal, they were constantly stopped for blocking by the director. Then they were asked to take their lines home and memorize them.

For the second scene, the same actors were given acting sides only. The action cues and word cues of the other actors were all they had to work with. There were no stage directions given. During the first rehearsal, they were occasionally coached **Share the stage picture!** Lines were not taken home to be memorized.

At the next rehearsal, the difference was remarkable. During the first scene, set rigidly from the outside, the actors neither saw their stage nor heard their fellow players as they struggled to remember cues, lines, and stage directions. They were concentrating on remembering, and their fears of not performing well produced physical tensions. Bodies could not move freely. The stage movements of these unskilled actors under such imposed conditions could only be stiff and awkward — what is commonly called amateurish.

□ *While it is sometimes necessary for a stage direction to be given to the actor, it must be translated into an integrated experience. That is, blocking must become an organic response to stage life. The following dialogue was with a ten-year-old player:*

Why did you go upstage just then?
"Because you told me to."
Isn't that mechanical?
"Yes."
Why do you think you were directed to go upstage?
"I went upstage for Tom to enter."
Why couldn't you wait for him where you were?
"I wasn't part of the scene going on at the moment. I have to be out of the scene, but I can't leave the stage."
What can you do standing where you are, out of the scene, and still be part of the stage picture?
"I'll put my focus on listening for Tom to come in."

The second scene, though more complicated in its demands, did not trouble the actors. Intent upon each other and with nothing to remember, they were free to solve the problems that came up or were posed by the director. There was no performing, there was only sharing.

Actors with many months of workshop training behind them will be able to translate any directions given by playwright and director into the necessary stage action. But the lay actor who in play after play is directed rigidly, step by step, with every movement plotted by someone else, cannot hope to discover personally the stage movements (blocking) required. The fear and tensions that were part of the first rehearsals and all subsequent playing have been memorized along with the lines and stage directions and have become a part of that which keeps the player in the past (memorizing) rather than the present (process).

The director who wraps actors up in yards of imposed movement and inflections until they cannot walk or talk is the same director who places the burden of stupidity or no talent on them when they cannot function on their own. One may bemoan the actors' inability to loosen the ties that bind them, but it is the director, in reality, who has secured the knots.

□ *Rigid players are often the product of a rigid director.*

Sight Lines for an End Stage

It is essential to emphasize the visual tie between the actor and the audience. A vocabulary of stage positions needs to be acquired.

Have players stand in specific places on stage: ***Downstage center! Upstage left! Downstage right! Upstage center! Center stage! Upstage right!*** Point out the line of sight between the individual player on stage and the individual in the audience.

To increase awareness of perspective, have players place their hands a few inches from their faces, and note how the objects beyond their hands, although larger, are almost obliterated from view.

Stage Picture

STAGE PICTURE is possibly best played at the start of the walk-through rehearsal as the warm-up. Many interesting moments occur on stage when players, in attempting to share the stage picture, must literally move others. (Avoid coaching players by name.) If some are not aware of the stage picture, other players must move them. If this does not happen, then all must move into a new stage picture around the unaware player. This awareness of each other creates groupings which are continually alive.

It is also important to demonstrate that when any part of you is visible, *you* are visible. Ask players to pull a piece of hair away from their heads, extend the heels of their feet, raise arms above their heads. Stage blocks, risers, and ramps are useful in helping to find interesting and different stage pictures.

The visual depth that is revealed in STAGE PICTURE, spontaneously arrived at by the players' recognition of the phenomenon, produces an extraordinarily vivacious and exciting stage picture. In a production of Shakespeare's *A Winter's Tale* directed by Andrew Harmon, STAGE PICTURE was played in rehearsal. A reviewer commented, "... the performers all remained on stage — as crowds, as an audience, as villagers, even as a storm — in a simple but effective series of shifting compositions."

□ *Avoid premature blocking; set nothing until well into rehearsals.*

□ *Any part of you is all of the part!*

□ *After* STAGE PICTURE *the most resistant (solo) player will accept and understand sidecoaching.*

□ *The actor, like a lithe ballplayer, always alerted to where the ball may land, moves around the stage aware of fellow actors as well as of the characters and parts played within the total stage environment. He or she is so sensitive to blocking that the stage picture is kept interesting and the sight lines clear in every moment of playing.*

STAGE PICTURE

Purpose: To recognize that any part of you is all of you.

Focus: On group creation.

Description: Players move in and out and around each other. When you call out *Stage picture!* players must instantly *hold.* If some part of each and every individual is not visible to the audience, continue to sidecoach *Stage picture!* Players instantaneously become visible. Some get down on their knees, others raise their arms; elbows appear. Many interesting and random formations result.

Variations: 1. Continuous moving stage picture: group stays in constant movement, keeping visible at all times.
2. Players move in and out and around one another. Sidecoach calls one player by name. All other players follow this one player until *Hold!* is sidecoached. Repeat with other players.
3. Two teams, one observes. As each stage picture is frozen, audience team infers a Who/Where/What from the players' positions.
4. Try this game using risers and ramps.

Stage picture!
Continue!
Stage picture!
Continue!...

Var. #1: *Stage picture!*
Stage picture!
Stage picture!...

Var. #2: (Name one player):
Hold!
(Name another player): *Hold!*

Audience, how did you reach your conclusions?
Players, how does your sense of the stage picture match what the audience saw?

Stage Business

The most skilled director or actor cannot always intellectually find interesting stage business. This must often be stimulated when neither actor nor script is helpful. Sometimes you will receive inspiration from actors at the moment it becomes necessary and will spontaneously select what is appropriate for both player and scene.

Both director and actor must understand that stage business is not just random activity to keep actors occupied. Like blocking, it should be integrated, alive, and free. Sidecoach: *Help your fellow player who isn't playing!*

☐ *Playing the games will bring up more business than could be found in many hours of solitary work on the script.*

Keep That!

During rehearsals, when something comes up that is *just right* for the scene, emotion, or character, side-coaching **Keep that!** at the moment the move, gesture, or sound appears has value for the actor, particularly when this occurs at a heightened moment.

I was directing a one-act play set in a coal-mining town in the early twentieth century. A mother sitting at a table in her kitchen speaks of her fear for the only male member of her family left to her. The others — husband, another son — died in unsafe mines run by unscrupulous owners.

A whistle blows. Fear mounts in the mother. A neighbor rushes on stage bringing news. We learn that her last son has indeed become another tragic victim. Her whole family has been sacrificed. In our production, the mother, upon receiving the news, did not sound agonized enough. At the next rehearsal, I went up on the stage without being noticed.

At the moment of receiving the news I gave her a strong punch in the back. She yelled out at both the surprise attack and the pain.

Keep that!

She did. In every succeeding performance. Physical pain — emotional pain — are the cries so different?

☐ *It is not recommended that a director cause physical pain to players. However, an occasional inspired shock might produce a very alive moment.*

Chapter 4:
THE SECOND REHEARSAL PERIOD

This is the digging period. As the actor develops actions through the exercises or in the reading of the script, the director may pick them up, enlarge them, and add something more, if necessary. The play is more or less blocked; almost everyone is completely off lines. Relations and roles are clear.

During this period it is necessary to establish and maintain the proper tone at rehearsals. All of the following pointers will help:

1. This must be the beginning of self-discipline. No chit-chat in the wings or in the theater.

2. If the groundwork has been well laid, you — as a fellow player — move directly to stage action with no danger of intruding on the actors' extensions or a static, dead quality appearing. You can cajole, shout, plead, and give exact steps without developing anxieties or stopping spontaneity. There will be no danger of hampering the stage work of individual actors.

3. Some games used earlier can be continued here if necessary. GIBBERISH, p. 53, and SLOW MOTION, p. 26, are valuable for digging up more stage business as are EXPLORE AND HEIGHTEN, p. 47, and BEGIN AND END, p. 46.

4. Your energy (the director's) must be high and apparent to the actors.

5. Watch for signs that your cast is growing stale and correct them quickly. Keep your cast moving, interacting, transforming.

6. Work for more heightened characterization. Nuances of blocking and business are important to note also.

7. Pursue spot rehearsals thoroughly. Go over a scene again and again. Use BEGIN AND END, p. 46, and SHADOWING, p. 76.

8. If the full cast can meet only three times weekly, the director should work *daily* in spot rehearsals.

9. The director must begin to build scenes one upon the other. Each scene has its own beginning and end, but every succeeding scene must build on the one before it. They are like a series of steps — each a bit higher than the last — as they rise to the play's climax.

10. Work outdoors whenever possible during this period. The need to rise above outdoor distractions seasons the players.

11. Have players rehearse barefooted and in shorts (climate permitting). You can then watch full-body actions (particularly the feet) and tell quickly whether a player is mouthing words or physicalizing the stage situation.

12. Listen to the players as well as watch them. Turn away from the stage and concentrate on dialogue alone, taking note of superficial readings, sloppy speech, etc.

13. You should not allow a sense of urgency to cause you to stop run-throughs. Keep notes on action that can be gone over again. Remember, there is plenty of time.

14. If players seem to be working at odds with you, you would do well to check the overall theme. Is there one? Are the cast and the director walking the same path?

15. Final acts have a way of taking care of themselves. Give most of the work and spot rehearsals to the earlier acts. If relationships and character are well established, the last act will need only the resolving of the play.

16. Some scenes may have to be gone over dozens of times for them to move smoothly. Others may need very little work other than the regular rehearsals. Any scene that has special effects must not appear awkward in performance, even if it means hours of work.

17. This can be a trying period or a fun period for everyone. Intense work can be exhilarating as cast and director get inside the script and themselves as well.

The Relaxed Rehearsal

The relaxed rehearsal gives perspective to the players. You should wait until everyone is off lines.

The players lie on the floor with eyes shut and breathe with strong emphasis on exhalation. Walk around, lifting a foot or a hand to make certain that muscular relaxation and release are complete.

The players then go through the lines of the script with eyes closed, *continuing to focus on visualizing the stage, the other actors, and themselves in the scene.*

□ *Sidecoach:* **See the ceiling! The floor! The walls! See outside the windows!**

The actors' voices become quiet and almost sleepy. In spite of the past work, old reading patterns and anxieties will often recur in rehearsals. But the relaxed rehearsal, coupled with the visualization of the stage, usually eases players' tensions and worries about the mechanics of their action, lines, cues, movement, etc.

Quietly remind actors not to mouth the others' words but to *hear* them, to keep focus on *seeing* the stage with eyes closed.

□ *Quietly sidecoach:* **Movement! See yourself! See fellow players! Be aware of colors! See the space between!**
— *whatever sidecoaching is appropriate for you.*

Players continue to speak lines. This sidecoaching will help players see the stage in full dimension, color, and movement, and to be hyperconscious of everything that takes place.

If properly handled and prepared for, this time will be enjoyable to all. The onstage work will be heightened and the last vestiges of anxiety will usually disappear.

General Improvisations around the Play

When it becomes necessary to provoke the actors beyond the lines of the script and to sharpen relationships, general improvisation is most helpful. General improvisations will seem to have no direct relation to the written play. They are presented, however, to give the actors insight into the characters they are playing.

In a production of *The Emperor's New Clothes*, a version written by Charlotte Chorpening, it became a problem to establish the relationship between the villainous, browbeating, cheating minister and the long-suffering weavers. It was solved by stopping rehearsals and doing an improvisation with Nazis coming to (Where) a village during the Second World War. The weavers took the parts of (Who) villagers, the minister and his entourage played the Nazi soldiers. The Nazis marched in, billeted themselves, herded people together, established authority, and used physical violence against those who protested. The villagers wept, fought, and shouted in vain. All the emotions necessary for the play came forth and were heightened. It was never necessary to rehearse these relationships again.

In the foregoing example, the reality of the historical scene had to be shaped into the structure of the play, but the intensity was never lost. Audiences were moved by the strength of these scenes and were astonished that "mere children" could give such amazing portrayals.

The following games are useful for improvisation around a text.

□ *Once the quality needed for a scene is captured, it remains (with rare exceptions).*

□ *General improvisations often give actors an insight beyond the words of the script by helping them "to see the word" and achieve a focus for the scene.*

—BEGIN AND END WITH OBJECTS—

Purpose: To help players recognize an *appearance* (ahh!) as distinguished from an act of mime.

Focus: On an object.

Description: In this three-part exercise, a single player decides on a small space object, such as a candy bar.

Part 1: Player performs a simple activity with the object (e.g., taking off the paper wrapper and biting into it).

Part 2: The player then repeats the activity, this time calling out "Begin!" each time a fresh contact is made with the object, and "End!" when each detail is completed. (See example below.)

Part 3: Finally, player repeats the activity as in Part 1 as fast as possible, without calling out "Begin!" or "End!" Begin series again.

Notes: 1. If Part 2 is done fully, each detail will be like an individual frame in a strip of movie film.

2. Sidecoach players to do the "beginning" and "ending" with great bursts of energy.

3. Part 3, the speedup, will be much clearer and sharper than Part 1, first, because of the detail created by "begin" and "end" and second, because the players have no time to recall these details. There is immediate contact with the object.

Example of Part 2: Player touches candy bar: "Begin!"
Grasps bar: "End!"
Starts to tear paper: "Begin!"
Tears the paper: "End!"
Begins to crumple paper: "Begin!"
Crumples paper: "End!"
Is ready to toss it away: "Begin!"
Tosses it away: "End!" etc.

Strong on "Begin!"
More detail!
More energy on "End!"
Break the action down more!
Call out with energy!

Players, which of the parts (first or third) best brought the object into the space?
Audience, do you agree?

SEEING THE WORD

Purpose: To stimulate fuller sense perceptions.

Focus: On the event being narrated.

Description: Single player. Player goes on stage and describes an actual experience, such as taking a trip, watching a football game, or visiting someone. The player maintains the focus (on the event) all during the sidecoaching. It is very important to continue narrating while receiving the coaching.

Notes: 1. As greater perception is awakened by side-coaching, note at what moment player begins to leave the *word* and relate to the *scene.* The speaking voice will become natural, the body will relax, and words will flow. When a player is no longer depending on words but is focused on the environment that was entered, then all artificiality and stilted speech disappear. A past event has become a present-time experience.

2. This exercise is very useful for the actor with long speeches and helpful for using words with more dimension.

Focus on the color!
The sounds! Weather!
People! Smells!
See yourself!

Did this scene feel real?
Were you hand in hand with the narrator on the trip?

EXPLORE AND HEIGHTEN

Purpose: To open the gate to new discoveries.

Focus: On being open to exploring, heightening, and expanding onstage play.

Description: Teams of two or more players agree on Where, Who, and What and play the event (scene) alert to sidecoaching as it is given.

Notes: 1. *Explore and heighten!* can be used as side-coaching throughout rehearsals. It is supportive, increases the energy level, and defeats the tendency to interpret or invent, which bogs down a scene.

2. Director must be totally attentive, watching and listening for sounds, movements, ideas, pauses, etc., which ordinarily might slip by unnoticed. The simplest gesture is explorable, alerting everyone to the possibilities for inspired stage life.

Explore that idea!
Heighten that feeling!
Expand that gesture!
Explore that sound! That object!
That thought!
Heighten it!

Players, did anything happen when players were coached to explore and heighten?
Players, did sidecoaching come out of what was happening, or was it imposed?

Laughter in Rehearsal

During the second rehearsal period actors are usually quite free from early tensions. Social aspects of the rehearsal are important, stage business is working, and everyone begins to have more fun. Fun, however, must be understood as the pleasure of working within the play and with the other players.

When laughter is moderate and enjoyable, it is useful. It most often denotes a breakthrough. It will help, not impede, the work. When it has elements of hysteria in it, however, it will prove destructive and must be carefully handled. You will, in time, listen to laughter and know what it means, much as a parent is able to recognize each separate cry of his or her child.

Sometimes, when laughter breaks out among the cast in rehearsal, release it by joining in the joke. However, if the laughter is uncontrollable, recognize the danger sign, stop the scene, and go on to something else.

Young players and older lay actors will often say, "He makes me laugh!" But it is important to point out that "he" or "she" never makes them laugh. It is lack of focus, for whatever reason, that causes the trouble.

Whatever causes it, laughter is energy, and players can learn that its physical impact on the body can be rechanneled into other emotions. Sidecoach: *Use your laughter!* Players will respond. Laughter can readily be turned to tears, tantrums, "play" laughter, and other physical action.

☐ *See uncontrolled laughter and wisecracking during rehearsals for what it is.*

☐ *Hysterical laughter is a sign of fear.*

☐ *Laughter sometimes is a means of pulling away.*

Seasoning the Players

We speak of players as being "seasoned" when they stand in good relationship to their part, the play, the set, the audience, and fellow players.[1] They have ease of movement, flow of speech, and above all, timing.

One of the most common weaknesses of the lay theater is the awkward, rough level of performance given by many of its players. While much of this roughness can be attributed to inadequate experience and training, other factors are also involved.

How often are most players on stage? Their work, for the most part, is directed toward one date, one production, and when that moment has passed, the experience ends. This abrupt breakdown in group expression thwarts growth just when it should be blossoming forth.

□ *Stopping the process stops seasoning.*

For the group interested in developing a repertory company, the seasoning that takes place during performance is especially valuable. But, between the problems of rehearsal time and the technical and mechanical difficulties which most community theaters face, there is little opportunity for gaining insights into the play and accomplishing the desired seasoning.

The following suggestions, if carried out, will round off many of the rough, uneven edges.

□ *No director can expect to get fully seasoned players in a short period of time.*

1. Plan a long time-span for rehearsals.
2. Use theater games during rehearsals.
3. Do not allow the players to take their lines home too soon.
4. Use stage picture whenever possible.
5. Create a tension-free, pleasurable atmosphere during rehearsals.
6. Bring in costume pieces and props early in the rehearsals.
7. Work to have players meet every crisis (off-balance moment) and adjust to sudden changes.
8. Break dependency on words.
9. Have a weekly run-through of the whole show throughout the second rehearsal period.
10. Schedule as many performances as possible. Perform to many different audiences, in a variety of places.

[1] See notes on Stage Picture and. accompanying game, pp. 39-40.

The Nonstop Run-Through

The nonstop run-through is especially valuable to the director with a limited amount of rehearsal time. It is, simply, a complete run-through of the play *without stops of any kind*. It is sacred; under no circumstances break in. Notes for spot rehearsals, pointers for individual players, and places in the individual acts that need more work can all be jotted down and cleaned up at a later rehearsal.

The mechanical problems which the director faces in getting the cast and play together during the first rehearsal period are so time-consuming that a nonstop run-through would be impossible during that time. Indeed, working on just one act of a three-act play usually takes most of the daily rehearsal at this stage. But in the second rehearsal period, when blocking (stage picture), relationships, character, integration, etc. have already been roughed in, the nonstop run-through should be scheduled as often as possible.

□ *Nonstop run-throughs strengthen the whole basic structure of the production, for the flow and continuity that they generate give the actors a sense of the movement and rhythm of the total play and help with the details of the scenes.*

Biographies

Toward the end of the second rehearsal period, ask the actors for biographies of their characters. This device occasionally brings some insights to the player who seems to be getting nowhere with a part.

The biography is everything about the character being played. Actors write out as fully as possible: schooling, parents, grandparents, favorite foods, main ambitions, loves, hates, what entertains, how evenings are spent, etc. Then, add what brought the character to this immediate stage situation.

Some biographies may be sketchy, irrelevant, or superficial. Allow no discussion about them. Simply accept them as they are and use them for reference material if and when the need arises.

A biography written by a fourteen-year-old girl playing in a fantasy stated that she and the villain had gone to school together as children and that she had loved him very much. While logically this would have been impossible in the social structure of the play, this emotional

□ *Written analysis should not be done until the player is settling into the character. When done too early, it is harmful and creates quite the opposite effect, for it keeps the character "in the head" of the player and the tale is usually quite subjective.*

involvement gave her relationship with the villain another dimension. She was able to show a sense of former love for the character she now detested. The audience, of course, was never aware of this story, but it brought much greater depth to her work. (When these two players grew up, they married!)

Chapter 5:
TUNE-UPS

As rehearsals continue, certain problems will arise which need to be diagnosed and helped. The following games aim at enriching your production.

Reading Lines Naturally

The actor is often quite fearful about words, particularly the child player, whose anxiety grows out of unpleasant past experiences with reading. With the unseasoned player the inability to read lines naturally is evidenced as lines become words rather than dialogue.

The first step in helping players to lose this preoccupation with the lines is to preoccupy them elsewhere.[1] Give a theater game that will remove concern from the words and solve the matter for them.[2]

Gibberish, extended movement, dance movement, singing dialogue, contact, and postponement of memorizing lines are all designed to help players in this way. Players must come to sense that lines grow out of dynamic action and involvement. For players who read haltingly, give gibberish or ad-lib lines until relationships form.

GIBBERISH requires total body response to make a communication; it provides excellent games to use throughout the three periods of rehearsal. GIBBERISH (facing) quickly opens up the players and helps the director to see the individual potentials within the group. It physicalizes the relationships and involvements, has extraordinary value in developing spontaneous business and blocking, and gives many clues for procedure to the director.

In an experiment with a one-act play that had only eight hours of rehearsal time (using players with limited backgrounds), GIBBERISH was used four times, consuming two and one-half hours, or one-fourth of the rehearsals. The resulting performance had unusual vitality, and the cast handled the play with the ease of experienced actors.

When using GIBBERISH during rehearsals, take players who have not had workshop training through GIBBERISH.

☐ *In the struggle to pronounce words "correctly," discomfort is continuously in the foreground.*

☐ *Avoid direct reference to the cause of the anxiety.*

☐ *A scene that will not play in gibberish is a scene without interaction between the players; theater communication cannot be made through words; the actor must truly show.*

☐ *If employed early in rehearsals, GIBBERISH produces remarkable acceleration in every aspect of production.*

[1]See VOWELS AND CONSONANTS, p. 25.

[2]SPACE SUBSTANCE, p. 68; SPACE WALKS, pp. 101-3; and CONTACT, p. 57.

GIBBERISH: SELLING

Purpose: To feel the impact of an audience.

Focus: On communicating to an audience.

Description: Single player, speaking gibberish, sells or demonstrates something to the audience. Allow one or two minutes clock time per player.

Notes: 1. Insist on direct contact. If players stare or look over the heads of the audience, ask them to "pitch" their sale, until the audience is actually seen. "Pitching," as practiced in carnivals or department stores, requires direct contact with others.
2. Both audience and player will experience the difference when staring becomes seeing. An added depth, a certain quiet, will come into the work when this happens.
3. Allow a player to be the timekeeper who calls time at the halfway point and at the end.

Sell directly to us!
See us!
Share your Gibberish!
Now pitch it!
Pitch it to us!

What was being sold or demonstrated?
Was there variety in the gibberish?
Did the player see us in the audience or stare at us?
Was there a difference between selling it and pitching it?

GIBBERISH/ENGLISH

Purpose: To create the off-balance moment.

Focus: On communication.

Description: Teams of three — two players and a side-coach. Players choose or accept a subject of conversation. When conversation begins to flow in English, sidecoach *Gibberish!* and players are to change to gibberish until coached back to English. Conversation is to flow normally and to advance in meaning.

Notes: 1. GIBBERISH/ENGLISH is ideal for developing side-coaching skills within all age ranges. When playing is understood, divide cast into teams of three. Many teams, each with its own sidecoach, can play simultaneously. Give all team members a chance to sidecoach.
2. Regarding sidecoaching, if gibberish becomes painful for any player, immediately change to English for a time. This helps the player who withdraws from the problem.
3. The moment of change should be when the player is offguard, in the middle of a thought or sentence. In the off-balance moment, the source of new insights — the intuitive — may be tapped. What was hidden comes to the rescue.
4. GIBBERISH can be used in conjunction with a number of other games.[1]

Gibberish!
English!
Gibberish!
English!...

Did the conversation flow and have continuity?
Was communication maintained throughout?
Players, do you agree?

[1] See Spolin, *Improvisation for the Theater*, pp. 122-27, 226.

Memorization

In community theater, memorizing lines is usually considered the most important single factor in working on a role. In truth, it is only one of many factors and must be handled carefully to keep it from becoming a serious stumbling block to the actor.

Do not allow players to take their scripts home during early rehearsal. This may be confusing to the players, for many feel that line memorization is to be done immediately and gotten out of the way so that actual direction can begin. However, premature memorization creates rigid patterns of speech and manner which are very difficult (and sometimes impossible) to change.

Remember that someone may be waiting in the player's home to "help." What well-meaning friend or relative can resist the chance to find the "right" way for the actor?

Memorizing lines too early brings many anxieties; the fear of forgetting them is great. These anxieties cast a shadow over every performance.

Players may feel a bit concerned when they are not allowed to take their scripts or sides home during the early rehearsals, for even the youngest has associated working on a part with learning words (memorizing). You must be reassuring.

It is during rehearsals that actors free themselves from the very words they are seeking to memorize. When this freedom becomes evident, it is safe to send lines home with the actors. When actors are integrated and relating to all aspects of the theater communication, all are ready to memorize — in fact for most the job has already been done. You will find that all that is needed is to go over a difficult speech here and there.

If the groundwork has been laid properly, you will probably find all actors off lines before the start of the second rehearsal period. This method is particularly valuable for children, for whom the fear of reading and of not being able to memorize their lines often becomes a serious obstacle, keeping many from developing as players. See Special Run-Through, p. 79.

□ *It is important to remember that dialogue grows out of involvement and relationships among players.*

□ *The time between rehearsals is a fallow period. Let it lie quietly.*

□ *All elements of production must be learned simultaneously and organically.*

□ *Try taking the sides from the actors' hands during rehearsals. Surprise! — they will know their lines!*

Timing

Timing is perceiving, sensing. It is an organic response which cannot be taught by lecture.

The player cannot develop timing intellectually, since this is a skill which can only be learned through experiencing, through intuition. That is why rigid blocking and the mechanical following of directions won't work.

Only the most seasoned players are generally thought to possess timing. However, if "seasoned" applies to that player who has both self-awareness and the ability to attune to the scene, the other players, and the audience, then every player can develop some degree of timing. Try the multiple-stimuli THREE-WAY CONVERSATION, below.

□ *Timing is the ability to handle the multiple stimuli occurring within a setting. It is the host attuned to the individual needs of many guests. It is the cook putting a dash of this and a flick of that into a stew. It is children playing a game, alerted to each other and the environment around them.*

□ *When players begin to know that a play is dragging, cues are dropped, and stage action is not alive, timing is off.*

THREE-WAY CONVERSATION

Purpose: To develop alertness to multiple incoming data.

Focus: For center player, to hold two conversations simultaneously; for end players, to hold a single conversation with center player only.

Description: Three seated players. One player (A) is the center; the others (B and C) are the ends.

  B (end)   A (center)   C (end)

Each end player chooses a topic and engages the center in conversation as if the other end player did not exist. Center must converse with both ends, fluent in both conversations (responding and initiating when necessary) without excluding either end player. In effect, the center holds one conversation on two topics. End players converse with center player only.

Notes: 1. Rotate players by sidecoaching, *Next!* New players, one at a time, come up and take an end seat, bumping one end player to the center, while the center moves over to become the other end player.
2. Center player does not just respond to end players, but can also initiate conversation.
3. Where, Who, and What can be added.
4. Avoid questions which create two separate conversations instead of two simultaneous conversations.

Speak and hear at the same time!
Take your time!
No questions! No information!

Did players avoid asking questions?
Did A stop hearing one player while speaking to the other? Did end players pick up from each other? Did center player also initiate conversation?

Contact

We sometimes see plays where actors stay in their own little areas — afraid to touch, look directly at, or listen to each other. Strong contacts between players, when a hand really holds another's arm or an eye looks into an eye, make productions more alive, more solid. An audience is able to sense when real contact has been made. And the director should coach players on this throughout rehearsals.

CONTACT can heighten highly dramatic scenes. Here the actors cannot escape into dialogue and character, but must stand and be seen. This forces all actors to make finer choices of stage movement.

☐ *Contact may be made either through direct physical touch, the passing of props, or eye focus.*

☐ *Take time out to do a scene from the play as a contact exercise.*

——Eye Contact #1————————

Purpose: To make players *see* one another.

Focus: On making direct eye contact with other players and directing sight to the prop or stage area to which reference is made.

Description: Two or more players. Who, What, and Where are agreed upon.

Example: Mary enters the room to visit John. John: "Hello, Mary" (eye contact to Mary). "Won't you come into the room?" (eye contact to room). Mary: "Hello John" (eye contact to John). "Here's the book I said I'd bring" (eye contact directly to book). "Do you want it?" (eye contact to John).

Note: To get the heightened energy or extra focus, suggest that their eyes take a closeup as a camera does. Doing this at the moment of eye contact is good even though it may be exaggerated. In time actors will learn to integrate eye contact subtly with all their work.

See!

Did they solve the problem? Was extra focus (energy) given at the time of eye contact?

The complex CONTACT game has a dramatic turning point for many actors. Due to the necessity for physical touch, it develops a closer communication and a deeper relationship with fellow players.

—CONTACT—

Purpose: To force all players to rely directly on their inner resources. To give stage business variety. To help players see and be seen.

Focus: On making direct physical contact with each new thought or phrase of dialogue.

Description: Two or more players agree on Where, Who, and What. Each player is to make direct physical contact (touch) with a fellow player as each new thought or phrase is introduced. With each change of dialogue a direct physical contact must be made. Players are responsible for their own dialogue and contact. Nonverbal communication (nods, whistles, shrugs, etc.) is acceptable without contact. If contact cannot be made, there is to be no dialogue. (As a surprise to players, add more challenging rules as in sidecoaching for Parts 2 through 4.)

Notes: 1. Players resist contact out of fear of touching one another. This shows itself in irritation at having to find variety; in poking and pushing other players away; in trying to make contact through props; in using only the most casual, constricted contact (tapping on shoulders, etc.). Go back to earlier exercises emphasizing relationships, body movements, and space substance.
2. If players do not wait for the focus to work for them, they will fall into irrelevant ad-libbing, poke at each other instead of making contact, and invent useless activity. Use sidecoaching Parts 2, 3, and 4 when players least expect it to help players vary contact.
3. Suggest players take five minutes to make nonverbal contact with a family member or friend without letting the other know. Discuss the various responses players received.
4. CONTACT is discussed in much greater detail in *Improvisation for the Theater*, pp. 184-88.

Part 1: *Contact!* (Whenever players speak without touching.)
Vary the contact!
Be quiet if you cannot make contact!
Use your full playing area!
Play the game!

Part 2: *No contact twice in the same spot!*

Part 3: *No hands!*
No contact with hands!

Part 4: *No contact with feet!*

Was involvement between players greater because of contact?
Was there variety in the contact?
Did the contact come out of Who, or was it done mechanically?
Players, did you keep focus on making contacts or were you concerned with the activity and scene?

Contact with the Audience

Understanding the role of the audience must become a concrete part of theater work. For the most part it is sadly ignored. Time and thought are given to the place of the actor, set designer, director, technician, house manager, etc., but the large group without whom the efforts would be for nothing is rarely given conscious consideration.

The audience is often regarded either as a cluster of Peeping Toms to be tolerated by actors and directors or as a many-headed monster sitting in judgment.

The phrase "forget the audience" is used by many directors as a means of helping players relax on stage. This attitude probably created the fourth wall. Players may no more forget their audience than their lines, their props, or their fellow players!

Every technique learned by the player, every curtain and flat on the stage, every careful analysis by the director, every coordinated scene is for the enjoyment of the audience, our fellow players, the last spoke in the wheel which can then begin to roll, making the performance meaningful.

The audience is the most revered member of the theater. Without an audience, there is no theater.

When there is understanding of the role of the audience, connection and freedom come to the player. Exhibitionism withers away when players see members of the audience not as judges or censors or even as delighted friends but as a group with whom experience is being shared. The fourth wall disappears, and the lonely looker-in becomes part of the game, part of the experience, and is welcome. This relationship cannot be instilled at dress rehearsal or in a last-minute lecture but must be handled from the very first sit-down rehearsal: *Share the stage picture! Share your voices! Vowels! Consonants!*

EYE CONTACT #2

Purpose: To help actors "project."

Focus: On making physical, prop, or eye contact with every member of the audience during the course of the speech.

Description: Single player must sell, demonstrate, or teach something to the audience.

Note: The sidecoaching phrase, *To us!* is most important to use when players avoid eye contact with the audience.

To us!
Sell (teach, demonstrate) to us!

Did the actors make physical contact as well as eye contact with the audience?
Was contact made with every member of the audience?
Did players see and not stare?

Listening to the Players

At various intervals during rehearsal the director should turn away from the players and listen to them. This listening without seeing the players in action often points up weaknesses in relationship, uncovers lack of "seeing the word," reveals falseness of characterization, and shows up "acting."

Picking Up Cues

Slow cues cause a serious lag in a scene and can cause a performance to drag. Be attentive to the problem from the very first rehearsal.

Slow cues often are the result of the player caught in a loop of indecision — should I or shouldn't I? In workshops use multiple-stimuli exercises such as active traditional games.

If the problem persists, slap hands simultaneously with the cues. SHADOWING, p. 76, can be used to encourage quicker uptake. Or have the slower player deliberately top the other's lines, cutting off the last few words. Sidecoach: *Now! Now!*

Handle cue pick-ups naturally by having players respond to action cues. Do not handle this mechanically. If it becomes necessary to work on word cues, wait until the latter part of the second or early third rehearsal period.

□ *Caution players that picking up cues does not mean faster speech. If a speech has a slow tempo, then it remains slow, even though the cue itself is picked up on time.*

Physicalization

A primary concern is to encourage freedom of physical expression in the actors. The physical and sensory relation with the art form opens the door for insight. Why this is so is hard to say, but be certain that it is so.

A player who can dissect, analyze, intellectualize, or develop a valuable case history for a part, but who is unable to assimilate it and communicate it physically, finds his understanding of the role useless in the theater. It does not bring the fire of inspiration to those in the audience. The theater is not a clinic, nor is it a place to gather statistics.

When a player learns to communicate directly to the audience through the physical language of the stage, the whole organism is alert. The player lends himself or herself to the scheme and is carried by this physical expression into direct communication — a moment of mutual perceiving with the audience.

A young player with a serious problem of monotone speech was asked to describe a flood he had witnessed.[1] Coaching him to see color, to focus on motion, sound, etc. had little effect. But when asked how he felt *inside* when he saw the water, he replied that he had a "funny feeling in his stomach." The "funny feeling" became the basis for sidecoaching during his talk, and the changes were immediate. As he focused on the fear of drowning, animation came into his speech. He had been unable to recognize the fact that he had fear. Asking him for an emotion provoked no response. But asking him how he felt *inside* (physically) enabled him to focus on his physical feeling and made it understandable to everyone.

☐ *Physicalization keeps the actor in an evolving world of direct perception — an open self in relation to the world.*

☐ *All life springs from physical relation, whether it be a spark of fire from a flint, the roar of the surf striking the beach, or a child born of man and woman. The physical is the known, and through it we may find our way to the unknown, the intuited, and perhaps beyond to the human spirit itself.*

☐ *The artist must draw on and express a world that is physical but that transcends the physical, a world that is more than the eye can see!*

[1]He was playing SEEING THE WORD, p. 47.

The two games below (SHOWING EMOTION THROUGH OBJECTS and CHANGING EMOTION) use objects as a means to help players physicalize emotions. These games are continuously useful during rehearsal. The section following deals with emotion more directly.

SHOWING EMOTION (INNER ACTION) ———— THROUGH OBJECTS

Purpose: To physicalize emotions.

Focus: On using a real object, selected spontaneously the moment the player needs it, to show a feeling or relationship.

Description: Two or more players. Where, Who, and What agreed upon. All objects are on a table easily accessible to all players on stage without disturbing the set or their stage movement. Substitute or add items to the following sample list of possible objects needed:

balloon	bell	sandbag
feathers	ball	egg beater
chains	rubber band	triangle
jumping rope	bean bag	party toys
trapeze (or swinging rope)	horn	ladder

Examples: 1. Where = bedroom. Who = three sisters, two older and one younger. What = two older sisters are dressing to go out; younger sister wishes she could go along with them. The two older sisters discuss their anticipation of the evening's fun. They throw balloons, blow feathers, and jump rope. The younger sister, bewailing the fact that she cannot go with them, walks around the bedroom weighted down with a sandbag, which she sometimes puts on her shoulders and sometimes drags along the floor.

2. A love scene between a bashful couple makes use of a ball rolled back and forth between their feet.

Note: This game gives unusual nuances to actors, even those with small amounts of training.

Variation: Players repeat same scene as above but use no objects.

Use the objects!
Use them!
Blow the balloon!
Jump the rope!

Did the objects follow the action?
Did the players retain the quality of the scene when they worked without the objects?

——CHANGING EMOTION————————————

Purpose: To physicalize emotion.

Focus: On showing emotion or feeling states through use of space objects.

Description: Single player completes an activity with focus on showing a definite feeling through use and handling of objects. Then the activity must be reversed, and player proceeds to undo what has been done, showing the changed feeling through the same handling and use.

Example: A girl dresses for a dance, showing pleasure or apprehension by the way she takes her dress from a closet. After learning the dance is cancelled, she shows disappointment or relief by putting the dress back in the closet.

Notes: 1. At the turning point, the director can ring the phone or send another player to provide the necessary information.

2. If changing emotion or feeling is shown only through facial mannerisms, players are "acting" and have not understood the meaning of physicalization. Using props and body is essential.

3. Games using objects to show inner action are continuously useful during rehearsal.

Physicalize that thought!
Explore and heighten
that object!

Was the activity identical before and after the turning point?
Was the feeling communicated through body changes?
What does pleasure do to one physically?
What does disappointment create kinesthetically?

Emotion

Breathe your vitality and life force into the character, not your emotions or sentiments. *Play* your *character's* emotions or sentiments. The following games should be played after the players have started to develop their characters.

── CHANGING INTENSITY OF EMOTION ──

Purpose: To help players work directly, physically, with emotion.

Focus: On changing the emotion from one level to the next.

Description: Two or more players. Where, Who, and What agreed upon. Emotion must start at one point and become progressively stronger. The sequence might run from affection to love to adoration, from suspicion to fear to terror, from irritation to anger to rage.

The emotion can also run in a circle, concluding back at the original emotion (e.g., affection to love to adoration to love to affection). However, this must be accomplished only through sidecoaching. It is very difficult to name the different emotions. You might prepare a list of emotions to look for.

Example: An act of betrayal by someone loved and trusted. The emotion is carried through a full cycle by sidecoaching. Players respond emotionally in the following order:
self-pity▸ anger▸ hostility▸ guilt▸ grief▸ sadness▸
affection▸ love▸ self-responsibility▸ understanding▸
self-respect▸ admiration for each other.

Notes: 1. Work very closely with the players, taking your cue from them as they pick up their cues from you. Follow the follower.

2. If the group is ready, these scenes can produce very exciting energy. However, if the scenes end up in mere chit-chat, the actors need more foundation work and/or side-coaching.

Both of you are in the emotion! Heighten it! More!
(The new emotion begins to arrive during the heightening.)
Deepen the feeling! Expand it!
(Immediately sidecoach new emotions as they arrive.)
The emotion is all around you, between you and in both of you!

Were the players acting (emoting) or showing (physicalizing)?

── CAMERA ──────────────────────

Purpose: To perceive stage life fully.

Focus: On putting full focus and energy on the other player.

Description: Two players. Who, What, Where agreed upon. Director calls out the name of one player at a time who puts head-to-foot focus on a fellow player. Activity is not to stop, but to continue throughout these camera changes, as director calls upon each player.

Notes: 1. In explaining the problem, use the image of becoming a camera — or suggest that the player is one large eye (from head to foot) to help actors in concentrating and focusing their energies on one another.
2. Well-timed sidecoaching is essential.
3. During rehearsals, calling *Camera!* produces valuable results.

Full-body attention!
See with the back of your head!
See with your viscera!
(Name one player, then another.)

Did the players give total bodily attention?
Did they see their fellow player with their feet?
Did stage activity continue?

Silence before Scenes

If actors appear urgent, rushed, overactive, or throw themselves into scenes without thought, have them sit quietly on stage before beginning to rehearse. While focusing on exhalation, and blanking out imagery, they are to sit quietly for as long as necessary. Stage action will begin whenever one of the players gets up and starts it.

Silence on Stage

In the SILENCE games, players are not to substitute subvocal or unspoken words but to focus on the silence itself and learn to communicate through it. An advanced group of players often arrives at uncanny clarity on a nonverbal level of communication.

SILENT SCREAM

Purpose: To show full-body response to a scream.

Focus: On feeling emotion (inner action) physically.

Description: Players are seated. Ask the group to scream without making a sound. When they are responding physically and muscularly as for a vocal scream, coach them to **Scream out loud!** The sound will be deafening.

Note: This game not only gives actors a direct experience to remember but is very useful for rehearsing mob scenes.

Scream with your toes!
Your eyes!
Your back!
Your stomach!
Your legs!
Your whole body!
Scream out loud!

Were you doing it or were you "acting out"?

SILENT TENSION #1

Purpose: To help players use silence to build tension.

Focus: On the silence between players.

Description: Two or more players (two preferred) agree on Where, Who, and What. Tension between players is so strong they are unable to speak; there is to be no dialogue during this event (scene). Where, Who, and What must be communicated through the silence.

Examples: 1. Elderly couple hearing a burglar downstairs.
2. Miner's family waiting for news after a mineshaft disaster.
3. Two sweethearts who have just broken their engagement.

Notes: 1. If the focus is understood, this problem necessitates eye contact and is therefore useful for players who "hide."
2. Sometimes coaching **Give and take!** is useful here.
3. True silence creates an openness between players and a flow of very evident energy, making it possible for players to reach into deeper personal resources.
4. Often tension rises between players culminating in a single scream, laugh, or some sound. Do not tell this to players. The player who says "I wanted to scream but thought you didn't want us to" was not focusing on the problem but on what the director wanted.
5. There is to be no inner dialogue (silent words) as well as no speech. All speech is to be held in "no motion."

Focus on the silence!
Communicate through the silence!
"No motion" on the inner dialogue!
Look at one another! See one another!

Did we know where players were?
Who players were?
Did players use inner dialogue?
Did players communicate through silence?
No words?
Players, do you agree?

—SILENT TENSION #2——————————

Purpose: To show the power of nonverbal emotion.

Focus: On the silence between players.

Description: Two players at a real table. No Where, Who, or What.

Notes: 1. Use of a real table is essential, giving players a support. This exercise usually produces a mounting emotion, strongly felt.

2. Sidecoach in a very soft voice, so as not to intrude on the silence. This becomes a most intimate threesome as the director softly stresses silence.

Keep silence between you. Silence around you. Silence within you. Above you. Keep the space between you silent.

Theatricality

The theater must be theatrical, of the theater. Real? Beyond the real. In fantasies, fairy tales, musicals, comic opera, dance theater, science fiction, Shakespeare, Paul Sills' Story Theatre, this beyond-the-real is deliberately worked for through special effects, lighting, sound, costumes, music, scripts. It is a world where every human predicament, riddle, or vision can be explored, a world of magic where rabbits can be pulled out of a hat and the devil himself can be conjured up and talked to.

Alive players keep the theatrical vibrant as well. The following theater games give players a specific experience of heightening and extension. Frequent use in workshops will bring greater exploration of possible stage action to the director and the script: EXPLORE AND HEIGHTEN, p. 47, SINGING DIALOGUE, p. 26, SPACE Games, pp. 100-3, EXTENDED SOUND (below), and SLOW MOTION, p. 26.

□ *The theater is a transcending, expanding experience for everyone, players and audience alike.*

EXTENDED SOUND

Purpose: To heighten and extend theatrical experience by showing that sound (dialogue) occupies space.

Focus: On keeping the sound in space between players and letting it land in fellow player.

Description: Two or more partners sitting a distance apart.
1. All players send a sound to all other players.
2. Each player sends a sound to each fellow player.
3. Give and take sending a sound to fellow players.

Notes: 1. Extended sound extends the moment.
2. The words of the script may follow extended *sound*.
3. This game could be used in the first sit-down rehearsal period.

No words! Keep the sound between you!
Keep the body upright!
Send forth the souuund!
Extend any physical movement!
Keep the sound in the space!
Let the sound land! Extend the souuund! Sloooow motion!
Speed it up as fast as you can!
Normal speed! Keep the space between you!
Extennnnd the souuuund!
Give and take!

Did players keep the sound in the space between them?
Did the sound land?
Did players physically extend the sound? Did players give and take?

Out of the Head! Into the Space!

When coached during playing, this phrase is not fanciful but produces an actual playing field, *space*, upon which the energy exchange, the playing, takes place between players. **Out of the head and into the space!** is recommended both for sidecoaching and for evaluation periods. The youngest player personally responds to and clearly senses this new invisible area, *space*, as real! Players accept the question, "Was it in your head or in the space?" without the need for defending their actions. **Out of the head and into the space!** does away with or prevents conditioned responses, clears the head, the mind, the intellect, of subjective, good/bad, right/wrong attitudes without need for analytical, psychological prying.

□ *Full-body perceiving/sensing equipment is strengthened and energy flow is easily available for use in all areas of daily needs as well when director and players and eventually the audience stay out of the head and get into the space.*

—— SPACE SUBSTANCE ——————————————————

Purpose: To sense space.

Focus: On the space substance between palms of players' hands.

Description: Part 1: Divide group into two teams — players and audience. Using the first team, each player working individually, have them move hands up/down, close together/far apart, and every which way just so long as palms are always facing. Players are to focus on the space substance between palms.

Part 2: With teams of two players, players stand opposite each other, three or four feet apart, and face the rounded palms of hands out towards the palms of fellow player. Players are to move hands up/down, closer together/farther apart, and keep focus on the space substance between the four palms of their hands.

Notes: 1. This exercise quickly gives players an experience of space substance. However, in time players must let partial focus on palms of hands dissolve in order to feel head-to-toe freedom to handle, play with, and respond to this most unique substance.

2. Audience team players will benefit from watching this game. However, if time is short, the full group may play this exercise simultaneously.

Part 1: *Move hands back and forth! Anywhere!*
But keep palms always facing!
Focus on the space substance between your palms!
Let palms go where they will!
Feel the space substance between!
Move the space substance about between your palms!
Play with it! Let it thicken!

Part 2: *Turn and face a partner!*
Two palms facing two palms of partner!
Feel the space substance between the four palms!
Play with the space substance!
Move it about! Heighten it!
Use your whole bodies!
Focus on the space between your palms and let it thicken if it does!

Did players let focus on space substance work for them?
Audience players, was space substance in players' heads or in the space?
Players, do you agree?
Did space substance begin to thicken for you?

Chapter 6:
THE THIRD REHEARSAL PERIOD

This is the polishing period. The jewel has been cut and evaluated and now it must be put into its setting. Discipline must be at its highest. Lateness to rehearsals and failure to read the call board or to check in with the stage manager must be sternly dealt with.

The organization of backstage work must begin as early as work on stage. Members of prop, sound, and lighting crews all must be just as attentive to time and responsibility as the actors, and this must be built up rehearsal after rehearsal.

☐ *You are preparing your players for a performance in which a late actor or a misplaced prop could ruin the whole show.*

Growing Stale

There are two points at which actors may grow stale: one is during rehearsals, the other is during a run of performances.

Sometimes this is because of a serious weakness in the basic structure of the production; at other times, it may be just a temporary setback. Sometimes the choice of material is poor, and you find yourself working with such a superficial text that it responds only slightly to your work. Sometimes actors have ceased to "play," and spontaneity and creativity have been replaced by rote and repetition. Or the actors may have lost focus and begun to generalize their relationship (Who) and their settings (Where). Rehearsals, like the play itself, should have a growing developmental theme and climax.

Several factors may account for the cast going stale during rehearsals:

1. The director has set the play too definitely from the outside, giving every movement, every piece of business, every voice inflection to the actors.[1]
2. Actors have memorized lines and business too early. Character, blocking, etc. were set before relationship and involvement developed.[2]
3. Actors have been isolated too long from the other aspects of production and need a "lift."

☐ *Staleness is a sign of grave danger. When actors become mechanical and lifeless, something has gone wrong.*

☐ *Staleness may be a sign that the director has neglected to plan the rehearsal time carefully to build maximum inspiration and excitement for the actors.*

[1] See p. 67 (*Out of the Head . . .*)
[2] Try GIBBERISH, p. 53 and DUBBING, p. 71.

Bring in a set piece, a costume part, or a prop. This opens up new vistas for the actors and builds greater vitality for the production.

4. Actors need more fun or play. This can be handled through rechanneling your attitude or by using games. This is particularly true of children and lay actors, where it may take much workshop before their involvement with the theater problems generates enough energy to hold interest without outside stimuli.

5. Players with limited backgrounds are certain they have reached their goal and achieved characters — they want the performance to begin. Sometimes only one or two cast members may be having difficulties. It may be that they do not like their parts or feel they should have had larger ones.

Other problems that usually lead to staleness during performance:

6. Imitating previous performances.
7. Being seduced by audience reaction.
8. Never varying performance. Try general improvisation around the same set (Where), characters (Who), but with a different activity (What).
9. Giving "solo performances." Play PART OF A WHOLE, p. 72.
10. Players getting lazy and sloppy.
11. Players losing detail and generalizing objects and stage relationships. Use VERBALIZING THE WHERE, pp. 73-74, when this occurs.
12. Players needing director's guardianship.
13. Play needing pick-up rehearsals.

For example: a problem arose during a player's second performance. It was at a settlement house, and the actor was a neighborhood man who did a brilliant piece of work when he stood up to the villain of the play. After the first performance he received thunderous applause. The next performance there was *no* applause. He was perplexed and wanted to know what had happened. "The first time you played, you were really angry, and we all knew it. In the second show, you were only remembering

□ *The theatrical atmosphere in the third rehearsal period should be heightened.*

the applause." He thought for a moment, nodded his head, and as he rolled up his sleeves and flexed his arms, he said, "Wait till I get him tonight!"

DUBBING

Purpose: To break speech patterns set too early and to produce new directions and playing capabilities.

Focus: On following the follower, with the voice of one player and the body of another player becoming as one whole (single) player.

Description: Two or three players (Subteam A) choose players of same sex to be their voices (Subteam B). This whole team (Subteam A plus Subteam B) agrees on Where, Who, and What. The voice players gather around a microphone with a clear view of the playing area, where the body players go through Where, Who, and What. The voice players reflect the onstage activity through the dialogue. The body players move their lips as if speaking, but are to use silent gibberish; no attempt to mouth exact words! Both subteams follow the follower in voice and action. Have the voice and body players exchange places and continue the same Where, Who, and What or choose a new one.

Notes: 1. At first, the separate players will become one body/one voice only in flashes, but when the connection is made, a burst of power rises between and through players, uniting them in true relation. Allow ten minutes of playing time before reversing teams.
2. If this connection does not take place and the voice simply follows the body's moves or vice versa, play more MIRROR and SPACE games, pp. 20, 92, 94-95, 100-3, until players experience what happens when they don't initiate, but follow the initiator, who is also following.
3. Sidecoaching is born out of what is emerging. The director does not demand, but acts as a fellow player, exploring and heightening what is seen and emerging.
4. When voice becomes one with onstage player's actions, onstage players get a sense of having actually spoken the words. Onstage players are not to be used as puppets by the dubbers; time must be allowed for onstage activity to emerge.
5. When dubbing works, two players experience true union and become as one player.

Stay with each other!
Avoid anticipating what will be said!
Reflect only what you hear!
Move your mouth in silent gibberish!
Don't initiate!
Follow the initiator! Become one voice! One body!

Did voice and body become as one?
Audience, do you agree?

──Part of a Whole, Object──

Purpose: To make players interdependent.

Focus: On becoming part of a larger object.

Description: One player enters the playing area and becomes part of a large object or organism (animal, vegetable, or mineral). As soon as the nature of the object becomes clear to another player, he joins as part of the whole. Play continues until all are participating and working together to form the complete object. Players may assume any movement, sound, or position to help complete the whole. Examples include a machine, cells in the body, clockworks, abstract mechanisms, constellations, animals.

Notes: 1. This game is useful as a warm-up or as a close to a session, as it generates spontaneity and energy. Players often stray from the original "idea" of the first player, resulting in fanciful abstraction.

2. The director should use sidecoaching to help single players join in, those who fear they may be wrong about the object forming, or those who rush to join in without awareness of the whole.

3. This theater game is also widely used under the name MACHINE. Imitators took the train example from PART OF THE WHOLE (*Improvisation for the Theater*, p. 73), and limited the dynamics of this game to one small area. Part of a Whole can be many things indeed.

Use your whole body to become your part!
Join in!
Take a risk!
Become another part of the object!

What was the whole object?
What did you think it was before you joined?

VERBALIZING THE WHERE, PART 1

Purpose: To make players more open to their environment.

Focus: On remaining in the Where, while verbalizing every involvement, observation, relation, etc. in it.

Description: Teams of two players agree on Where, Who, and What and sit in playing area. Without leaving their chairs, players go through the event (scene) verbally, describing their actions in the Where, and their relation to the other players. Players narrate for themselves, not other players. When dialogue is necessary, it is spoken directly to the other player, interrupting the narration. All verbalization is in the present tense.

Example: Player 1: "I tie my red-and-white apron around my waist and reach for the cloth-covered cookbook on the table. I sit down at the table and open the book, looking for a recipe...."

Player 2: "I open the screen door and run into the kitchen. Darn it, I let the door slam again! *'Hey, Mom, I'm hungry. What's for dinner?'*"

Notes: 1. This exercise can aid in breaking players of opinions and attitudes in their work.

2. Do not go on to the next game unless players have understood the focus, and it has worked for them.

3. So-called observing is usually filled with personal attitudes (past) — seeing something through dos and don'ts, prejudices, assumptions, etc. — the very opposite of simply seeing what is at hand. Just seeing, right now! allows players, whether writing or speaking, to open as yet closed doors within themselves. Allow the invisible to become visible; surprise!

Keep it in the present time!
Verbalize the objects that show Where!
Describe other players for us!
Keep opinions out!
See yourself in action!
No information!
Keep objects in space!
Use dialogue when it appears!
Verbalize the way your hands feel on the chair!
No opinions!
That's an attitude! An assumption!

Did player stay in the Where, or was the player in the head (giving background information, judgments, opinions, attitudes)?
Players, do you agree?
Was there more that could have been verbalized?
Parts of the Where?
Parts of the action?

Verbalizing the Where, Part 2

Purpose: To make the invisible visible.

Focus: On retaining physical reality from Verbalizing the Where, Part 1.

Description: Same team, having played Verbalizing the Where, Part 1 while seated, now gets up and actually plays the event (scene) through. Players no longer verbalize their actions as in Part 1, but speak only when dialogue is necessary.

Notes: 1. If focus on remaining in the Where while verbalizing the scene (Part 1) has worked for the players, the Where with space objects should now seem to appear perceptible to all observers (the invisible becomes visible).

2. It is not necessary that every detail covered in the narration be part of the scene played.

3. If the narrative part of this exercise has dealt with what players are thinking rather than on the detail of the physical realities around players, Part 2 can become no more than a "soap opera."

4. Note the complete absence of playwriting in these scenes as true improvisation appears.

Keep the physical sense of the Where — smells, colors, textures . . . communicate it!
Do not tell us!

Players, did the first part of this game help give life to the onstage situation in Part 2?
Was the playing of the event or scene easier because of the verbalization?
Audience players, was greater depth brought to the playing of the event or scene?
Was there more life than usual?
More involvement and relation?
Players, do you agree?

Spot Rehearsals

As a rule it is best to schedule spot rehearsals in the third period, when the play has definite shape and flow. The spot rehearsal is utilized to give special time to working over a troublesome scene which has not resolved itself within regular rehearsals. It might be a simple entrance or an involved emotional scene. It might be a problem of achieving a more effective mob scene or helping a single actor explore and heighten a long speech.[1]

This type of rehearsal will often intensify a scene which has previously been weak. Let the spot rehearsals pull the players and you away from the generality of the overall play and focus on minute details. This quiet concentration and intimacy between players and you produces deeper insights for everyone.

☐ *While you may spend hours on a scene that takes but a few moments on stage, such attentive work on a selected bit or piece enriches the player's role and brings added depth to the play.*

Shadowing

Shadowing is similar to a spot rehearsal. The focus is on helping the actor explore and heighten the Who, What, and Where.

Pick someone needing help and follow that player closely on stage. Prior to doing so, explain that focus is to be kept, for if a player is amused or distracted by your shadowing, then the point of the action will be lost. Talk to the player being shadowed (since you stay very close, you can speak quietly without disturbing the others) and pick up the actions of that player as well as the others:

Force him to look at you! Contact! Physicalize that feeling! Slow motion! Pick up a (prop)! Let yourself be seen! Look out the window! Give/take! Listen to what is said! Look at the ceiling!

Use this particular technique, as you use the spot rehearsal, after players have been with their roles long enough for some seasoning to have taken place.

It will be valuable during rehearsal to have the actors shadow each other. Being a shadow sharpens sight and hearing.

☐ *Shadowing will help a player to visualize, to make contact, to move. It will also give you the actor's point of view.*

☐ *Like the closeup of a camera, shadowing gives an extra burst of energy through you to your actor.*

[1] See Explore and Heighten, p. 47, Begin and End, p. 46, and Seeing the Word, p. 47.

──SHADOWING────────────────────────

Purpose: To create artistic detachment.

Focus: On the Where, Who, and What.

Description: Teams subdivide. Where, Who, and What agreed upon. Subteam A plays the scene and Subteam B shadows them. Floorplan is known by all, actors and shadows alike. Shadows make continuous comment to the actors they are shadowing. During playing, sidecoach A and B to *Change!*

Example: Where = bedroom. Who = husband and wife. What = getting dressed to go out. As Subteam A goes through the scene, one member of Subteam B shadows the husband, and the other shadows the wife. The shadows should stay close to the actor and speak quietly so that the other actors and shadows do not hear.

Notes: 1. Shadows are not to direct, to take over the action, but merely to implement and strengthen the actor's physical reality at their own (the shadows') discretion.
2. Shadows can comment on inner action if desired. If scene becomes "soap opera," however, stop exercise and keep shadows commenting on the physical objects in the environment.
3. Caution: this is a fairly advanced problem and should not be given until the group members have already shown some degree of breakthrough and insight into earlier problems.
4. Have actors shadow their own characters during rehearsal.

Why does she always hog the mirror?
Do you see the brown flecks in her eyes?
Are you going to let him wear that tie?
The picture of your mother on the wall is crooked.
Why don't you help her zip up her dress?
Change! Change!

Exits and Entrances

An actor must integrate not only entering the stage but also leaving it. There must be heightened focus on the player's entrance or exit, if only for a fleeting moment. It is sharpness in framing such details that gives the stage clarity and brilliance.

Enter on your upstage foot, a direction commonly given to actors as a necessary rule, is simply used to keep players from *hiding* as they come on stage. This exercise suggests that there are many more exciting and challenging ways to meet an audience!

EXITS AND ENTRANCES

Purpose: To develop response to stage life.

Focus: On making exits and entrances to get full involvement with fellow players.

Description: Teams of four, five, or six players agree on Where, Who, and What. Each player makes as many exits and entrances as possible with Where, Who, and What, but each exit or entrance must be so framed that onstage players are fully involved with the player's entrance or exit. If players barge in or out without the full involvement of fellow players, audience players are free to call out: "Come back!" or "Go back! You didn't make it!"

Notes: 1. Devices such as shouting, stomping feet, jumping up and down, etc. may bring attention to the oncoming player but not the involvement with Where, Who, and What which is needed for the playing (process) to continue. However, if onstage players give attention and become involved in player's exit or entrance, no action is barred, no matter how fanciful it may be. Therefore, if exit or entrance involves Where, Who, and What, players may crawl out, dance in, fly out again, or enter with a quiet "hello."

2. EXITS AND ENTRANCES should organically make clear the difference between getting attention (an isolated player) and becoming involved (part of the whole).

3. Homework: Ask players to take note when entering a room how often people (themselves included) are satisfied with attention rather than involvement.

Keep onstage movement!
Don't plan your exits!
Watch for the moment!
Stay with the activity!
Play the game!
Let exits (entrances) come through Where, Who, and What!

Which exits and entrances truly had full involvement and which were only trying to get attention! Players, do you agree?

Seeing the Show

There comes a moment when you see all the aspects of the production integrated. There will suddenly be rhythm, pace, characterization, fluidity, and a definite unity. Many scenes will be far from finished, costumes may still be in the sewing stages, and a few players will be moping around, but it will seem, on the whole, a unified piece of work. You must now clean up rough spots, strengthen relations, intensify involvement, and make alterations.

☐ *You may see this unified show for an instant and then not see it again for a number of rehearsals. But this is no cause for concern. It was there and it will come again.*

There are few directors who are completely satisfied with their productions. Particularly when working with young people and unseasoned adults you must be aware of their capacities. If you are not satisfied with the production because of the limitations of your actors, you must nevertheless realize that at this stage of growth it is all that you can expect. If there is integrity, playing, life, and joy in the performance, your show will be well worth viewing.

☐ *Once you have gained this insight into your show, you must accept it, even if you feel it should have been different.*

Stage Fright in the Director

If you do not accept your show at this late date your own emotional problems will intrude on the actors. By now, you are getting stage fright, concerned with whether the audience will accept and like your presentation. This feeling must be hidden from the actors.

☐ *The very process of doing a show has a great deal of natural excitement. If you add a feeling of hysteria to this, the actors will catch it.*

During this period, you may be short-tempered. Explain this to the players, warning them that you may be gruff during the integration of the technical aspects. Response will be most sympathetic. A director who worries about the actors until the last minute, hoping to squeeze a little more out of them, will not help the play in any way.

☐ *One way to prevent stage fright is to give the production over to the technical aspects of the play in the last hours of rehearsal.*

The Special Run-Through
(Cutting the Umbilical Cord)

There are no mistakes on stage as far as the audience is concerned, for they usually do not know the script or the action of the play. And so a player need never let the audience know when something is amiss.

The special run-through puts the cast completely on its own. Developed for child actors, it works equally well for adults. It goes as follows. At a regularly scheduled run-through of the play (just prior to dress rehearsal), tell the cast that in the event of a break of any kind (laughter, lost lines, etc.) by one of the actors, all — the full cast — must cover up and keep the scene going. Failing to do so, all go back to the beginning of the act. If, for instance, an actor breaks at the very end of the second act and no one has covered this, the director quietly calls, "Begin the second act, please!" and the actors must go back over the ground they have just covered.

After a few "begin agains" you will find the cast descending upon the culprit who made the break. Remind everyone that all are equally responsible for keeping the play going and they must cover for fellow players in case of trouble.

This is the fullest expression of the group experience at work. The individual players must be very disciplined, for they are now directly responsible to the group (the play). At the same time it gives a deep sense of security to the player to know that no matter what happens on stage, and whatever crisis or danger, the group will come to one's aid for the sake of the play.

The special run-through is very exciting for the players and keeps all of them on their toes, alerted for that moment when it may become necessary to cover up for a fellow actor. After one or two rehearsals, the show will go on even if the very roof should fall in.

□ *The audience knows only what the actors show them.*

□ *The presence of the director at the special run-through is not to harass or punish, but simply to function for the last time as part of the group. The special run-through cuts the umbilical cord between the director and players.*

Makeup and the Actor

This is a good time to have character makeup sessions, especially if the play is a fantasy which requires something unusual. Time spent in applying makeup and allowing players to experiment with their own characters will aid their work on stage. Just as lines must become a part of the player, so must makeup. It is far better to have all players develop their own makeup, with an assist from more experienced artists, than to have it applied for them.[1]

After one or two sessions, have players make charts of their own makeup to keep for reference. If makeup is handled as a developing factor in the total fabric of the theater experience, children as young as six can learn. Makeup, like a costume, must be worn easily and with conviction, not be used for the first time on the day of the opening performance.

Makeup must not totally mask the player, or merely make a face pretty, giving the player a facade to hide behind. Recognize makeup as an extension of character, not the basis for it. Eliminate heavy makeup, particularly with young actors playing older roles. This keeps the actors thinking of themselves as players, and forces them to rely on their performing skills.

□ *It was not an unusual sight at the Young Actors Company to see a seven-year-old helping a five-year-old to apply makeup, although it was our guess that at home, the seven-year-old couldn't even comb her own hair properly.*

The Costume Parade

It is advisable to run the costume parade together with a makeup rehearsal. Briefly, the parade is just that: a grouping of players, completely dressed and made up, so that you can see how they look under the lights. Changes can be made quickly if necessary, and everything should be looked at for fit, comfort, etc. If there is no time for a costume parade alone, it may be combined with a rehearsal. Schedule it, if possible, at a time when players will be fresh and free from other commitments. This time should not be squeezed in. You may need a good number of hours to complete the dress parade, depending upon the type of show and the number in the cast.

□ *The costume parade can help make the last week a joyous, relaxed time instead of an anxiety-ridden one.*

[1] See p. 13, for an example of how a clown helped players. Many professional companies bring in makeup experts.

The First Dress Rehearsal

A first dress rehearsal must be kept as free from tension and hysteria as possible, despite all the confusion which it may bring. It may indeed seem a bit lifeless, but this partial let-down is far better than a rehearsal in which chaos reigns.

Under no circumstances may the first dress rehearsal be stopped once the curtain goes up. As with the run-throughs, the director must take notes as the acts progress and have a meeting with the cast after each act to discuss sight-lines, roughness, etc. Limit yourself to discussion of those things which can be altered without disturbing the past work. You must have faith in yourself and in your players. The first dress rehearsal for any play is usually discouraging, but a second dress will follow, as well as the preview before an invited audience, to pull the show together.

A community theater director once visited the Young Actors Company at a dress rehearsal. She was surprised to see the director down at the mouth because of the poor dress rehearsal. "You should feel elated," she said. "Your actors are all off their lines!" This is indeed a sad state of affairs when the bogey of knowing the lines determines the whole quality of a performance.

□ *There is an old theater superstition that "a bad dress rehearsal means a good performance." This is an obvious excuse to keep everyone from becoming discouraged.*

□ *If you do not "have a show" at the first dress, you will not get one by overworking the actors during the last hours.*

The Performance

The performance brings to its fruition the whole creative process of doing a play, and the audience must be involved in this process. The audience is the last spoke which completes the wheel, and its relation not only to the play but to the playing is most important. Audience response can help you evaluate your production.

No one can use an audience for self-glorification or exhibitionistic reasons. If this is done, everything you and your actors have worked for will be destroyed. On the other hand, if the whole concept of sharing with the audience is understood, the players will give exciting performances.[1]

Laughter from the audience often causes a player to lose focus. This distorts the player's relation to the

□ *The mark of a fine actor is his or her response to an audience. It is desirable to give as many performances as possible to allow this response to be developed in the players.*

□ *Remember to strive for audience appreciation of the play as a whole and not of just one or two of the players or the set or the lighting and special effects.*

[1] See Contact with the Audience, p. 58.

whole, as each performance becomes a means to achieve
the laughter again. Here the player is working only for applause. If this persists, the director has somehow failed
the player.[1]

Random Pointers

1. During the show, stay away from the backstage
   area. Everything must be so well organized that
   it runs smoothly without you. Messages can
   always be sent backstage, if necessary.
2. Be certain that costumes are always well but-
   toned and sitting right. Runners who are
   worried about whether their shorts will hold up
   are not free to run!
3. Be relaxed and pleasant around the cast if you
   drop into the dressing room.
4. Have one run-through between performances if
   possible, unless they are nightly. If this is not
   possible, a short talk after each performance will
   help to eliminate the few bits of roughness or
   sloppiness that may be appearing here and there.
5. A short pick-up talk prior to performances may
   be necessary from time to time.
6. Pick-up rehearsals during the run of the show
   help actors keep focus on problems in the play
   and prevent them from becoming lazy and
   generalizing. Rehearsals also bring greater
   clarification of random flaws and intensify the
   good work that already exists.
7. Players must learn to allow the audience full
   laughter. Begin early with the simple rule of
   allowing laughter to reach its peak and then
   quieting it by a gesture or movement before
   beginning the next speech.
8. Backstage discipline must be observed strictly at
   all times.
9. The players will grow in stature during the performances if all factors allow them to do so. The
   stage is the X-ray picture where everything
   structural shows up. If the play is presented

[1] See Growing Stale, p. 69.

shabbily, if its "bones" are weak, this will be seen, just as any foreign objects show up in an X-ray. False and dishonest characterizations and relationships become apparent. This can be explained and stressed for the players whenever necessary.

10. Workshops and rehearsals may not produce *fully* seasoned players in their first show, but all will be well on their way.

11. If, toward the end of the run, actors decide to "cut up," remind them that their last performance is the audience's first. Enjoyment must come from the performing itself, not from cheap, sophomoric tricks on fellow players.

Chapter 7:
GAMES FOR CONTINUING REHEARSALS

Many facets of your production develop simultaneously. What game to choose? Remember, character is intertwined with emotion; blocking with relationship. Working on one develops the other. However, some games can be used for specific purposes.

Interaction between players and director (audience) produces high energy flow. This interaction is produced by the connection among players in the (stage) space evoked through the game's focus with and through skillful sidecoaching.

Interjecting theater games in a rehearsal that is going nowhere brings refreshment to both the players and you. While for the most part you will select games that help solve the problems of the play, sometimes games independent of the play generate energy in the players and aid in the maturing or seasoning process. Every rehearsal should make use of at least one theater game.

When playing theater games, all props and set pieces must be space, not material. The playing area needs only chairs or small benches. Aside from helping to make the invisible visible, these space objects can be put to extravagant or exotic use.

Character Games

Although it may be tempting to present and discuss character in early rehearsals, it is best to wait until players appear to be fully in contact with each other and involved with the script. Character can grow only out of personal integration with the total stage life.

Premature attention to character on a verbal level may throw the actor into static role-playing (acting), preventing moving relations with fellow players. Instead of reaching out into the stage environment, the player will be acting out private needs and feelings, will be mirroring the self, and will be giving an interpretation of a character, an intellectual exercise.

□ *If a role is to be truly played, character must not be defined in a lecture which is independent of involvement in stage action.*

In the unskilled player this will be quickly uncovered, but it is far more difficult to catch in the more clever and skilled actor. Always keep players from "acting" (performing) in their early work, by stopping rehearsal if necessary. Ask them, "Were you acting?"

In early rehearsal, avoid discussing character except in the most casual way, on a simple Who basis (relationship).[1] Remember, since most actors know that character is the essence of theater, this absence of direct character discussion may be very confusing until all begin to see character emerge out of the stage life and its relations and realize that "acting" puts up a wall around a player. An actor must see and relate to a fellow actor, not a "character." We play football with other human beings, not with the uniforms they are wearing.

Developing a character is the ability to intuit an essence from the complex whole person. This ability to show the essence, rather than a description of the detailed whole, springs spontaneously from within.

How much better to think of the actor in this way, as a human being working within an art form, than as one who has changed personality for the sake of a role in a play!

The following group of theater games deals with the problem of character on a physical, structural basis from which a character may emerge. Absorb the WHO games carefully so as to be able to present them at the time when they will most effectively act as a series of simple steps toward character development.

□ *Character must be used to further theatrical communication, not as withdrawal.*

□ *May an actor assume outward physical qualities to get a feeling for a character or must he or she work through feelings to get the physical qualities? Sometimes a physical attitude or expression will give us an intuitive jump.*

□ *A person becomes the physical expression of a life attitude. How many of us can pick out a doctor, a public-relations person, a schoolteacher, or an actor in a crowd?*

Physical Visualization

The use of images in getting a character quality is an old and tried device and can sometimes bring a totally new dimension to a player's role. Images can be based on pictures or any object, animate or inanimate, that the actor chooses.

Such images should be used only when the character development has not evolved from the total stage relation. Players who have had some experience with this way of working are eager to begin work on the character

[1] See the WHO games, pp. 88-89.

immediately and sometimes set about taking some image privately without letting the director know. This can become a serious handicap, for the director and actor may be at odds with one another.

Using images is, however, useful in emergencies. Once, for example, a girl was asked to step into a small part on a few hours' notice, because of the sudden illness of the regular actor. She was playing in another one-act play on the same bill. In rehearsal it was soon evident that she could not easily shake the characteristics of the other role, those of a shy, frightened girl. The new part was a portrayal of a perky, talkative woman. By suggesting she take an animal image, specifically a turkey, the director enabled her to project the necessary qualities for the role almost immediately.[1]

☐ *The director may be working to get rid of the very mannerisms the actor is hanging on to because of the image the actor has created.*

Box Full of Hats

Purpose: To help a player rapidly establish a character (Who).

Focus: On quickly selecting costume pieces for character quality.

Description: Teams of two or more players. This game can be played in either of two ways: players agree on Where, Who, and What and then pick costume pieces from the box full of hats to fit the scene. Players may also pick costume pieces at random, allow the costumes to suggest character qualities, and then choose Where, Who, and What based on their selections.

Note: Your box of hats is simply as many costumes, costume pieces, and small props as you can readily collect: old gowns, jackets, a chef's hat, a sailor's cap, an Indian headdress, helmets, shawls, capes, blankets, sheets, paper wings, tails for animals, gloves, canes, eyeglasses, pipes, umbrellas, etc. Hang clothing, blankets, and sheets on a rack with the box full of hats nearby. Old neckties can be used as belts, making it possible to use any size dress or coat by taking up extra length and girth.

Variation: Once players have randomly selected and donned costumes, audience players determine Where, Who, and What for players.

Share your voice!
Keep objects in space — out of the head!
Show! Don't tell!
Let the character qualities support you!
Become part of the whole!
One minute to play!

(To audience players):
Did costume pieces help or hinder the players' Where, Who, and What?
Players, do you agree with audience players?

[1] See Animal Images in *Improvisation for the Theater*, pp. 262-64.

How Old Am I?

Purpose: To establish early orientation to character.

Focus: On showing a chosen age.

Description: Establish a simple Where, such as a corner bus stop, with a bench in the playing area. Each player works alone on the problem. If time is short, five or six players may be at the bus stop at the same time. However, players are not to interact in any way. Each player chooses a particular age (perhaps writing it on a slip of paper and handing it to the director before going on). Players enter the playing area and, while waiting for the bus, show audience players how old they are.

Note: Players will tend to act out their old frames of reference, which is expected within this game. Play How Old Am I? Repeat, p. 90, in the same session if at all possible so players can discover the difference between "acting out" and allowing the focus to work for them.

Show us your age!
The bus is a block away!
It's coming closer!
It's here!
(If you wish player to explore further possibilities): *It's held up in traffic!*

How old was this player?
Player, do you agree with audience players?

What Do I Do for a Living?

Purpose: To show the availability of hidden resources.

Focus: On the chosen occupation.

Description: Teams of five or more. Each player chooses an occupation, writes it on a slip of paper, and hands it to the director. Player enters the playing area and waits, focused on occupation. Players do not know one another and avoid dialogue.

Notes: 1. The evaluation should provoke insights into physicalizing character. It should be most casual. Later games will allow other insights into playing character.
2. Jokes, "acting," and clowning are evidence of a resistance to the focus.
3. Allow several minutes for the effects of the focus to become manifest.

Variation: Mix up the occupations and pass them out at random to players just prior to entering the playing area.

Feel the occupation in your whole body!
Hands! Feet! Neck!
(When occupations begin to emerge):
Keep repeating your profession!
The bus is coming!

What were the occupations?
Did players show or tell?
Players, do you agree?
Is it only through activity that we can show what we do for a living?
Does the body structure alter in some professions (doctor or laborer)?
Is it an attitude that creates change?
Is it the work environment?

—WHO AM I?—————————————————————

Purpose: To build a character through showing, not telling.

Focus: On involvement in the immediate activity until the Who is revealed.

Description: Whole group or large teams. One player volunteers to leave the room while the group decides who player will be: for example, union leader, cook in the Vatican, circus barker, etc. — ideally someone who is usually surrounded by much activity or institutional life. Then the first player is asked to return and sit in the playing area, while the others, one at a time or in small groups, enter in relation to the Who and become involved in appropriate activity until the Who is known.

Notes: 1. The most difficult part of WHO AM I? is to keep the unknowing player from making it a guessing game and the others from supplying clues. Who will emerge if player remains open (in waiting) to what is happening and involved in the immediate activity.
2. Choosing famous people or historical personages should be avoided until the group is familiar with the exercise.
3. The exercise reaches its natural ending when the unknowing player shows by word or deed that Who has surfaced. Players may, however, continue the scene when Who is known.

Don't try to guess Who you are!
Let it emerge!
Assume nothing!
Relate to what is happening!
Relate with fellow players!
Ask no questions!
Who you are will be revealed!
Other players, give no clues!
Show! Don't tell!
Don't give it away!
No urgency! Wait!

Did the player try to guess Who or did he or she wait until it was communicated through relation?
Player, do you agree?
Did you rush the discovery?

—WHO GAME #1—————————————————————

Purpose: To show, not tell, character.

Focus: On allowing who you are to reveal itself.

Description: Two players, A and B. A is seated in the playing area. B enters. B has a predetermined character relationship with A, but has not told A what it is. By the way B relates to A, A discovers who A is.

Notes: 1. The game ends as soon as A realizes Who. But, if time allows, continue if there is involvement between the players.
2. After evaluation, reverse positions and let A choose a relationship with B.
3. If players tell instead of show, have players use GIB-BERISH, p. 53.

Show Where!
No questions!
Wait! No urgency!
Let Who you are reveal itself!

Did B show the relationship or tell?
Did A anticipate Who or allow Who to be revealed?

WHO GAME #2

Purpose: To show character through facial expressions.

Focus: On keeping many facial qualities while going through Where, Who, and What.

Description: Teams of two or more players. Who, Where, and What agreed upon. Players should choose a simple relationship and activity, such as husband and wife watching television. Have each player write on individual slips of paper a list of facial features and then descriptions of those features. The descriptions should be emotional rather than structural. Players should then make out slips for each facial feature. For instance:

lower lip — sad	upper lip — petulant
tip of nose — inquisitive	nostrils — annoyed
eyes — cheery	eyebrows — serene
forehead — forbidding	chin — belligerent
shape of face — saucy	

When the slips have been completed, separate them by features and put the slips into piles. Let each player pick one slip from each pile. The players are to take on as many descriptions as they wish and retain them while playing the scene.

Part 2: Play the game with structural qualities accompanying facial features.

nostrils — sinuous	cheeks — hollow
eyes — liquid	upper lip — stiff
eyebrows — heavy	forehead — overhanging
chin — double	nose — sharp

Note: It will be helpful to provide mirrors so players can observe physical characteristics when first taken on.

Players, did holding these physical aspects make you feel mechanical?
Did you gain any new insights?
Audience, did any of the players show a new character quality?
Did the facial qualities seem integrated with the scene?

—How Old Am I? Repeat—

Purpose: To tap the intuitive.

Focus: On the chosen age only.

Description: Players work alone on the problem, but five or six may be at the bus stop at the same time. Player sits or stands quietly waiting for the bus, focusing on the chosen age. When ready, what is needed to solve the problem will emerge for player's use.

Notes: 1. It is difficult for players to believe that the blank mind (free of preoccupations) is what we are after. If focus is on body-age only, all will have a unique experience as players become older or younger before our very eyes!

2. Many, of course, will rely on character qualities and role-playing, rather than allowing it to happen. Look for muscular release and shiny eyes as new sources of energy and understanding are tapped.

3. We all have stowed away countless characters. Repeating the age sends a signal into this vast storehouse, and by letting the focus work for us it delivers us a character quality fitting for our bodies. Hidden memory systems are called upon. Allow data to emerge.

Feel the age in your feet! Your upper lip!
Let your spine know the age! Your eyes!
Send the age as a message to your whole body!
(When age appears): *"Bus is a block away!"*
Repeat age over and over!
Observe! Let the focus work for you!

How old was the player?
Player, do you agree with audience players?
Was the age in your head?
Or in the body?

—Exercise for the Back #1—

Purpose: To communicate with whole body.

Focus: On using the back to show feeling or a state of being.

Description: Single player chooses an activity that requires sitting with back to the audience, such as playing the piano, doing homework, etc. Player is to communicate feeling or attitude with the back alone.

Note: Lead in to this game by having two players stand before the group. One faces front, the other turns away. Have group list parts of the body which can be used for communication. Ask players to move the part called. Front view: movable forehead, eyebrows, eyes, cheeks, nose, mouth, jaw, tongue, shoulders, chest, stomach, hands and feet, knees, etc. Back view: head (no movable parts), shoulders, torso (solid mass), buttocks, heels, backs of legs (comparatively immobile). Compare the number of movable (communicating) parts of the body when facing or turned away from the audience.

Keep the feeling in your back!
Not on your face!

Did player show with the back?
Could more variety of movement be found?
Was Who communicated? Age?

EXERCISE FOR THE BACK #2

Purpose: To communicate with the whole body.

Focus: On showing feeling or state of being through the back.

Description: Teams of any number of players agree on Where, Who, and What, which is played with backs to audience without dialogue.

Examples: Watching a game or fight; a waiting room.

Notes: 1. Do not expect too much at first. Only the more naturally skilled players will be able to give a complete expression. In time, all players will communicate with their backs.
2. Players can be made aware that the rule "Don't turn your back to the audience" is employed in the theater merely as insurance against loss of communication (sharing) with the audience.
3. This exercise is useful in rehearsal for crowd scenes.

Show us with your back!
Use whole back!
Feel it in your back!

Was Where, Who, and What communicated?
Did players keep focus?
Could there have been more variety of expression?

HOLD IT! #1

Purpose: To show how attitudes affect character.

Focus: On holding a facial and bodily expression through a series of Wheres, Whos, and Whats.

Description: Four players (even division of male and female desirable). Have players sit in playing area. Ask each to give a short statement of attitude such as, "Nobody loves me." "I never have any fun." "I never met a man I didn't like." "I wish I had nice things." Players are to work for a full facial and bodily expression of their phrase. When achieved, and body expression takes over, sidecoach **Hold it!** Players are sidecoached through a series of Wheres, Whos, and Whats. Players are to hold the physical expression of the attitude through all the changes.

Example: Sidecoach same team from nursery school to grammar school, graduation day, a double date, office party, card party, old people's home — the events of a lifetime.

Let the attitude affect your chin, eyes, shoulders, mouth, hands, and feet!

Were the basic expressions (attitudes) maintained, even if somewhat altered in each event (scene)?
How did these attitudes affect relationships? Manner of speaking?

—HOLD IT! #2—

Purpose: To show character and emotion through attitudes.

Focus: On maintaining a physical expression or bodily quality throughout Where, Who, and What.

Description: Teams of two or more players. Each player takes on a body expression, such as hunched shoulders, belligerent chin, petulant mouth, overhanging forehead, fixed stare in the eyes, pigeon-toes, firm aggressive step, flabby stomach, etc. Players then agree on Where, Who, and What and proceed while retaining their chosen physical expression or bodily quality.

Note: HOLD IT! games suggest to players that subjective emotions and their physical expression are often one.

Hold it! Hold it!
Share with the audience!
Hold it!

Did the chosen physical characteristics influence players' activities within Where, Who, and What?
Players, do you agree?

—MIRROR PENETRATION—

Purpose: To sidetrack players from the good/bad syndrome and free them for improvised speech.

Focus: On restructuring your face from the inside out to look like another.

Description: Players are paired with or choose partners with faces different from their own in structure. Each team of two players decides on a simple relationship (husband-wife, etc.) and chooses a topic for discussion or argument. Players sit facing one another and begin the conversation. When director calls the name of a player, that player assumes the partner's facial structure while continuing the discussion. When called on, players are not to reflect movement and expression of partner's face as in earlier Mirror games,[1] but rather are to attempt to restructure the face to look like the partner's. When partner's name is called, first player resumes his own facial structure. Players are to continue the discussion without stopping as director changes the "mirror" frequently.

Notes: 1. Players are thrown into an explicit talking relationship; however, both partners should be so occupied with penetration and restructuring faces that the problem of dialogue is taken in stride.
2. At first, players will show very little physical change in faces. This game has value despite this apparently modest result, since it forces players to look at another and *see*.
3. Players must penetrate each other's faces in order to rebuild their own to look like the other.

Rebuild your nose like partner's!
Jawbone! Forehead!
Change the mirror!
Focus on partner's upper lip!
Keep up the discussion!
Change the line of your chin!
Your jaw!
Change the mirror!
Exaggerate your partner's cheekbones! Keep talking!
Sculpture your face to look like partner's!
From the inside out!
Share your voice!

Did you penetrate facial structure, or simply reflect expression and movement? Audience, do you agree with players?

[1] See MIRROR, WHO IS THE MIRROR?, FOLLOW THE FOLLOWER, pp. 20-21.

—TRANSFORMATION OF RELATION———

Purpose: To allow players the exciting experience of the new relationships they are capable of playing.

Focus: On movement, constant interaction, relation between players within a series of changing relationships.

Description: Two players begin with a relationship (Who), such as a doctor examining a patient and, while playing, allow Who to transform into new relationships, one after the other. Players are not to initiate change (invent it) but are to "let it happen." In the course of changing relationships, players may become animals, plants, objects, machines and enter any space and time.

Notes: 1. When players are trapped in an event (scene) and are role-playing, sidecoach **Mirror each other!** to help reestablish the relations between players and thus get back on focus.

2. In every case the changing relationships reveal an event (scene) in microcosm before it shifts. The tendency is to stay with the new event (scene), but the moment it emerges is also the moment of transformation. For example, as the doctor examines the patient, the stethoscope, which is the object between the players, might transform into a snake or a bedsheet and the players find themselves in a new Where, Who, and What.

3. Dialogue should be minimized as TRANSFORMATION OF RELATION requires a great deal of body movement for the transformation to emerge. Often in playing, sounds will emerge — grunts, shouts, etc. Sound in this case is part of the rising energy and continues body movement, whereas dialogue (in this exercise) can stop this process by dealing with ideas instead of physical energy and can lead to role-playing. The goal is movement, interaction, transformation!

4. Sidecoaching must be done with extremely high energy.

Change!
Follow the follower!
Initiate fully!
Go with that sound! That movement! That look!
Explore that object between you!
Use your whole body!
Heighten that action!
Move! Change! Move! Change!

Players, did you invent or let it happen?
Were you able to keep focus on relation or were you trapped in the event or scene, or the relationship (role)?
Audience, do you agree?

Listening/Hearing Games

Do not make players overly conscious of speech variance. Through playing and sidecoaching VOWELS AND CONSONANTS, SINGING DIALOGUE, pp. 25-26, etc., speech will be cleaned up organically. To quote Marguerite Herman, co-author with her husband Lewis of manuals on dialect: "Unless a student has basic speech problems, no great change in pronunciation should be forced upon him. A 'cleaning up' and a 'toning up' should be all that is necessary."

——MIRROR SOUND——

Purpose: To communicate orally but nonverbally.

Focus: On mirroring partner's sounds.

Description: Teams of two players. Seated players face each other. One player is the initiator and makes sounds. The other player is the reflector and mirrors the sounds. When *Change!* is called, roles are reversed. The reflector becomes the initiator. The old initiator becomes the reflector who mirrors the new initiator's sounds. Changeovers must be made with no stop in the flow of sound.

Notes: 1. Sounds can be loud or soft, humming or shouting. Variety is desirable.

2. Teams of two players can gather in different spots around the room and all play this game simultaneously as director sidecoaches all teams at once.

No pause!
Notice your body/physical feeling as you mirror your partner's sound!
Change the mirror!
No time lag!
Keep up the flow of sound!
Feel how your body feels as you reflect sound!
Change!
Feel your legs! Your hands! Your shoulders!
Change!

─Mirror Speech─────────────────────

Purpose: To follow the follower verbally.[1]

Focus: On mirroring/reflecting initiator's words *out loud*.

Description: Teams of two players. Players face each other and choose a subject of conversation. One player is the initiator and starts the conversation. The other player is the reflector and mirrors *out loud* the words of the initiator. Both players will be speaking the same words out loud at the exact same moment. When ***Change!*** is called, roles are reversed. The reflector becomes the initiator of speech and the old initiator becomes the new reflector. Changeovers must be made with *no stop* in the flow of words. After a time, no more changes will be called by the director. Players will "follow the follower" in speech, thinking and saying the same words simultaneously and without conscious effort.

Notes: 1. Initiators should be coached to avoid asking questions. If a question is asked, the reflector must *reflect* the question, not *answer* the question.

2. The difference between repeating the words of the other and reflecting the words of the other must be understood organically before "follow the follower" can take place. In a sense, players connect with one another on the same word and become one mind, open to one another. As the conversation flows between players seemingly without effort, true dialogue appears!

3. The script itself can be presented and explored simply by restricting the subject of conversation between players to the subject of the script.

4. If time is limited, have group count off into teams of three players, one of which is the sidecoach. All teams play the game at the same time in different areas of the room.

Reflector, stay on the same word!
Reflect what you hear!
Reflect the question! Don't answer it!
Share your voice!
Change the reflector! Keep the flow of words between you!
Stay on the same word!
Know when you initiate speech!
Know when you reflect!
Change! Change!
(When players are speaking as one voice, without time lag): ***You are on your own! Don't initiate! Follow the initiator! Follow the follower!***

Audience players, did onstage players stay on the same word at the same time?
Players, did you know when you initiated speech and when you reflected speech?
Did you know when you were following the follower?
All players, what is the difference between repeating speech and reflecting speech?

─────────────────────────────────────

[1] See Follow the Follower, p. 21.

STAGE WHISPER

Purpose: To develop dramatic moments.

Focus: On stage whispering: on whispering with full projection and open throat.[1]

Description: Teams of two or more players agree on Where, Who, and What in which the players are forced to whisper to each other. For example, thieves in a closet, lovers quarreling in church. Just before calling curtain, players might sit and pant for a few seconds in the playing area.

Notes: 1. As this exercise requires a great deal of physical energy, the released energy brings alive, amusing, exciting stage situations, instant vignettes. If focus is kept on the stage whisper, this exercise almost invariably produces a theatrical experience for the players.

2. Calling out **One minute!** may heighten a team's effort in this exercise.

3. Reminder: Whenever players, because of audience response, get caught cerebrally on interesting dialogue or humor developing in the event (scene), sidecoach players back to the focus: **Stage whisper!**

Open your throat!
Use your whole body!
Whisper from the bottom of your feet on up!
Not a whisper . . . a stage whisper!
Share your stage whisper with the audience!
Focus on stage whisper! Stage whisper!

Did players talk low or did they use a stage whisper?
Players, did you let the focus work for you?
Audience, do you agree?

UNRELATED CONVERSATIONS

Purpose: To show that the full body is required in listening.

Focus: On extending *full-body attention* to the one speaking; never agreeing, disagreeing, or answering.

Description: Any number of players. Players sit in a conversational group. Any one player speaks on any self-chosen subject. All other players listen to what is being said, giving full physical attention to the speaker. Another player breaks in and starts another subject totally unrelated to the first conversation. While each player keeps his or her own personal subject going, many other conversations are started by different players. All players continue on their own subjects when breaking in.

Notes: 1. Body attention creates a flow felt among players. Sidecoach everyone who drifts away from the one speaking. Players are connected by body attention to one another and not by language or subject matter.

2. Use during sit-down rehearsal.

Give the one speaking your full body attention!
Pick up the conversation whenever you wish! Break in! Stay with your own unrelated subject!
No agreement! No disagreement! Physical attention! Listen with your feet! Listen with your eyes! Spine! Top of head! Shoulders!

[1] A stage whisper is not a true whisper. It must be heard by an audience.

——Vocal Sound Effects——————————————

Purpose: To create an environment using sounds.

Focus: On becoming the environment (Where) through sound effects alone.

Description: Teams of four to six players agree on Where and gather around a live microphone. Using sound as part of a whole, players become the chosen environment (a railroad station, jungle, harbor, etc.) Because there is no onstage action, players may stand out of sight of audience, or audience players may close eyes.

Notes: 1. Pass the mike around to allow individual players to experiment with the sound.
2. A tape recording of a team's work played back during evaluation adds to everyone's awakening. Excitement results when players recognize their individual contribution as part of the whole.
3. Allow use of cellophane crackling for fire, a straw in a glass of water for streams, etc. Encourage variety.

*(Usually not needed.) **Sound is your fellow player!**
Bring the Where into the space!
Give the sounds their place in space!
Each sound is part of the whole!*

*Where were the players?
Was the Where in the space or in the players' heads?
(Ask individuals): Were you part of the whole?*

——Who's Knocking?——————————————

Purpose: To develop nonverbal communication.

Focus: On showing the Who, Where, and What through knocking.

Description: One player remains out of sight of the audience and knocks on a door. The player is to communicate Who is knocking, for What reason, Where, time of day, weather, etc. Some examples might include a policeman at night, a rejected suitor at a sweetheart's door, a messenger from the king, a very young child in a closet.

Notes: 1. In evaluation, the director will find many observers did not know the exact circumstances, the Where, Who, and What, of a knock. Now that all know, have player repeat the knocking. Observers will listen more intently and find communication clearer now, when they do not have to guess.
2. Repeating the knock after evaluation keeps audience players part of the game and involved in what other players are doing.
3. Some questions in evaluation may be unanswerable but asking them may bring new insights to the players.

***Share your knock!**
Try it again!
Heighten it!
Let the sound of your knock enter space!
Hear/meet the sound in space!
Put full body attention on the physical sound!*

*Who is knocking? At what door?
What time of day?
For what purpose?*

No Motion Games

"No motion" is not a freeze. Its purpose is to create a resting or non-thinking area between people precisely when they are busy with onstage dialogue and activity. If done with understanding, out of the resting or non-thinking area energy comes bursting through and expresses itself in unique use of props, dialogue, more intense character relationships, and rising tension within the onstage scene.

What we are trying to make happen is the acceptance of the invisible as a connection between players. Connection is the real communication.

As the purpose of these games is to stop conceptual thinking and verbalization, avoid over-presentation.

□ *Some players find the directive, **Rest!** more useful to them than any other in achieving the physical feeling necessary.*

——No Motion Warm-Up——————————

Purpose: To aid in understanding elements of movement.

Focus: On the "no motion" within movement.

Description: Part 1: Players raise their arms, breaking up the flow of movement into a series of stills or frames as on a filmstrip.

Part 2: When so coached, players raise arms up and down in regular speed but focus on the periods (feeling) of "no motion" within the total flow of movement.

Note: Properly executed, this exercise gives a physical feeling and understanding of keeping out of the way. By focusing on "no motion," hands, legs, etc. move effortlessly without conscious volition. You are at rest in "no motion" — without attitude about the action.

Part 1: *Raise your arms as in a series of stills!*
Focus on the feeling of "no motion" as you raise your arms!
Focus on doing nothing!
Bring your arms down in "no motion"!
You stay out of it!

Part 2: *Raise your arms in regular speed, focusing on "no motion"!*
Triple your speed, focusing on "no motion"!
Up and down! Normal speed in "no motion"!
You stay out of it!

How many felt "no motion"?
The feeling the arms were moving themselves?

—NO MOTION: WALKING———————————

Purpose: To explore body movement.

Focus: On the "no motion" within movement.

Description: Players (full group if possible) walk around the room, play area, or any large area focusing on "no motion."

Notes: 1. All of the sight, hearing, and touching exercises can be added to this walk around the room if time and inclination allow. The sidecoaching directive, *No motion!* can be used for climbing, running, etc.

2. *No motion!* used as a sidecoaching directive keeps the player quiet and off the subject. This loss of concern releases fear, anxiety, and the like and leaves a clear, blank mind through which something new might come forth.

Walk around the room in "no motion"!
Focus on the periods of "no motion"!
You do nothing! Let your body walk around the room!
You stay in "no motion"!
As you walk around the room, let your sight go out into the whole room and see all the objects around you!
Continue! See your fellow players in "no motion"!
Let your body walk around the room in "no motion"!
Take a ride on your own body and view the scenery around you!

Space Games

The use of space objects is not mime. Space objects make the invisible visible: an appearance! Magical, spontaneous projections of our (invisible) inner self enter into the visible world! Mime prescribes a known gesture understandable to an audience.

With space objects, there is direct seeing through the intuitive. In mime, the audience interprets the gesture with the logical, rational mind.

☐ *In theater games, go for the appearance. Reach out and let the space object emerge!*

──Finding Objects in the──────
Immediate Environment

Purpose: To make the invisible visible.

Focus: On receiving objects from the environment.

Description: Three or more players agree on a simple relationship and a discussion which involves everyone, such as a PTA meeting or family conference. Discussion might take place around a space table. During the course of the meeting, each player finds and handles as many objects as possible. Players do not plan ahead what these objects will be.

Notes: 1. This is a two-way problem. The onstage occupation, the meeting, must be continuous, while the preoccupation, the focus, must be worked on at all times. Some players will keep the meeting going and neglect the focus. Sidecoach accordingly!

2. When this problem is solved, much to everyone's excitement, endless objects appear: lint is found on a neighbor's coat, dust floats through the air, and pencils come out from behind ears. All players have the opportunity to discover this for themselves.

Take your time!
Let objects appear!
Keep the discussion going!
Share your voice!
Keep in contact with each other!
The objects are found in the space!
Help your fellow player who isn't playing!

Did objects appear or were they invented?
Did players see each other's objects and use them?
Did players refer to objects or actually contact them?
Players, did objects come through association, or did you allow them to appear?

Space Walks

Using space or extended movement during rehearsals helps to integrate the total stage picture. Such exercises break the static isolation many players still cling to in spite of work on other acting problems. While especially useful for fantasy, extended movement exercises also do much for realistic drawing-room plays. Then try the opposite, No Motion, pp. 98-99. Exercises in using space substance, p. 68, parallel the use of dance or extended movement and can be applied during rehearsals.

This type of rehearsal helps players, young and old alike, to realize that the whole body, even while still, must always be ready to spring into stage action. This gives an interesting energy to the stage and often a choreographed quality appears. Consider the body parts — eyes, ears, brain — as physical structures or equipment through which space flows, carrying sight, sounds, etc.

□ *Like a dancer, an actor is never merely to wait for his or her turn while working on the stage.*

Space Walk #1

Purpose: To familiarize players with the element (space) they live in.[1]

Focus: On feeling space with the whole body.

Description: Players walk around and physically investigate space as an unknown substance.

Notes: 1. As in all space walks, the director walks with the group while coaching the exercise. Use your players' physical characteristics (tight mouth, hunched shoulders, etc.) as your guide to coaching space walks. For example, if one player has a fixed eye expression, you might say, **Put space where your eyes are! Let your sight pass through your eyes!** If you single out one player's area of tension, do not let that player realize it. What helps one helps all.

2. A simple introduction to space substance is to ask players what is between you and them. Players will respond with "air," "atmosphere," "space." Whatever the players call it, ask that they consider whatever is between, around, over, or under them as "space substance" for the purpose of these exercises.

3. Give some time between each coaching phrase for players to have the experience.

4. You may wish to delay trying these games until you are more comfortable with this approach to space.

5. Do not belabor evaluation of space walks.

Walk around and feel the space around you!
Investigate it as some unknown substance and give it no name!
Feel the space against your back!
Your neck!
Feel the space with your body and let your hands be as one with your body!
Feel space inside your mouth!
Along the outside of your body!
Feel your body shape as you move through space!
Now let the space feel you! Your face! Your arms! Your whole body!
Keep your eyes open!
Wait! Don't force it!
You go through the space and let the space go through you!

Did anyone get a feeling of space or of letting space feel you?

[1] See also Feeling Self with Self, p. 24.

SPACE WALK #2

Purpose: To feel surrounding space.

Focus: On holding yourself together or letting space support you, as sidecoached.

Description: Players walk around the room and hold themselves together to allow the space to support, as sidecoached.

Notes: 1. As in SPACE WALK #1, director walks with the group while coaching the exercise. Allow time between coaching phrases for the experience.
2. Letting space support you does not mean losing control or going limp. Player is to allow the body its proper alignment. *Allow your body its proper alignment!* is a useful sidecoaching phrase in this exercise.
3. Play this a few times. Everyone finds pleasure in it. Wait until players know one another.
4. Change back and forth between sole support and space support, until players experience the difference.

Variation: Have players close eyes and walk around each other. While eyes are still closed, sidecoach *Freeze!* Ask players to identify by name or description players around them.

You go through the space and let space go through you!
As you walk along, go inside your body and feel tenseness!
Feel your shoulders!
Up and down the spine!
Feel your inside from the inside!
Observe! Take note!
You are your sole support!
You are holding your face together! Your toes on your feet!
Your whole skeleton together!
You are holding your body together!
If you did not hang on to yourself, you would fall into a thousand pieces!
Now change!
Walk through the space and let the space support you!
Your body will understand!
Note your body feeling!
Put space where your eyes are!
Allow the space to support your face! Your shoulders!
Now change!
You are again your sole support!

Was there a difference between you as your sole support and allowing space to support you!

Var.: *No groping with hands!*
Feel, see with your whole body!
Keep eyes closed!

Space Walk #3: Skeleton

Purpose: To physically feel the body.

Focus: On physical movement of one's skeleton in space.

Description: Players walk through space focusing on the skeletal movement of bones and joints.

Note: Sidecoach players back to their own body form.

Part 1: *You go through the space and let the space go through you! Feel your skeleton moving in space! But avoid seeing a picture of your skeleton!*

Feel the movement of every joint! Allow your joints to move freely! Feel the movement of your spine! Your pelvic bones! Your legs!

Let your head rest on its own pedestal!

Feel your skull with your skull!

Now put space where your cheeks are! Around your arm bones!

Between each disk in your spinal column! Put space where your stomach is!

Feel your own form once more! The outer outline of your whole body in space!

Feel where the space ends and you begin!

Part 2: *Now pick up the body and facial attitude of another person!*

From the inside! The lips! The eyes! The skeleton!

Get the full physical expression of that person!

Now, take on the feelings (emotions) of that person! Keep the physical!

Did you feel your own skeleton moving in space?

—TOUCH AND BE TOUCHED/SEE AND BE SEEN—

Purpose: To help create greater sight and feeling in players.

Focus: On the sidecoaching.

Description: Allow players to move freely around the stage space.

Notes: 1. Remember to keep players moving and to allow time between sidecoaching directives.

2. Allow players to touch and be touched, see and be seen. It is difficult for many to allow themselves to be seen. Changing back and forth from *Occlude!* to *See!* helps.

3. *See and be seen!* removes attitudes, information, and narration about what the player is seeing. A direct experience takes place, clearing the space among players.

4. In *Take a ride on your own body!* players experience detachment, thus finding greater involvement.

Allow the space to flow through you and you flow through the space!
Allow your sight to flow through your eyes!
Allow the space to flow through you and your fellow player!
Take a ride on your own body and view the scenery around you!
Touch an object in the space — a tree, a cup, a piece of clothing, a chair!
When you touch the object, feel it, allow it to touch (feel) you! (Vary objects.)
Touch a fellow player and allow your fellow player to touch you!
Touch and be touched! (Vary players.)
See an object!
The moment you really see it, allow the object to see you! (Vary objects.)
See a fellow player! Allow the fellow player to see you!
Look full face at your fellow player and occlude: Do not see him or let yourself be seen!
Change! See and be seen!

Was it difficult to allow yourself to be touched . . . to be seen!

Traditional Games

A difficult problem arose in a cocktail party scene in which six or seven players had to mill around and socialize while surreptitiously watching for the high sign from their director to break loose and create bedlam. When the scene was rehearsed, it was static and un-spontaneous. The problem was finally solved through the traditional game WHO STARTED THE MOTION?, p. 28. After playing this game four or five times, the cocktail party scene came off, and the needed *looking without looking* quality emerged very sharply. The excitement released by the game was retained by the players throughout their performances.

Traditional games are especially valuable in cleaning up scenes requiring sharp timing. A park scene with passersby crossing and recrossing the stage (requiring continuous entering and exiting) created a serious timing problem. It was impossible to "set" the crosses through cues, since there had to be random crossing but never too many at one time. The traditional game OBJECT RELAY (below) solved that problem for the players. After playing the game once, it was repeated, but this time the players walked instead of running to the goal and back. As one or two exited, the others entered with no lag or dead spots.

Have a few good game books on hand at all times and be familiar with their contents for that moment when a stage problem might be solved with a traditional playground game.[1]

□ *Traditional games release a strong physiological response.*

□ *When you introduce a game, become a fellow player as often as possible.*

——OBJECT RELAY————————————————

Description: Two teams. Teams line up side by side. The first player on the team has an object in one hand (a rolled-up newspaper, a stick, etc.). The first player from each team must run to a goal agreed upon, touch it, run back, and hand the object to the next player on the team who must in turn run, touch the goal, run back, give the object to the third player on the team, and so forth until all players have finished and a team has won.

[1]Any of Neva Boyd's books are recommended.

When I Go to California

Purpose: To develop memory and observation.

Focus: On remembering a series in sequence.

Description: Teams of ten to twelve players in a circle.

Part 1 (the traditional game "When I Go to California"):
The first player says, "When I go to California, I'm going to take a *trunk* (or any other object)." The second says, "When I go to California, I'm going to take a trunk and a hat box." The third player takes a trunk, a hat box, and adds something new. Each player takes, in *exact order*, all that has gone before and adds a new object. If a player makes a mistake, that player cannot add an object and sits out until only one player is left.

Part 2 (the traditional game "When my ship comes in"):
Same team plays as above (with a new series of objects if desired), but instead of saying "take my shoes," for example, player acts out putting on shoes. The next player repeats the first player's acting out and adds a new one. Thus player will put on shoes and perhaps play a flute. Each player repeats, in order, all that has gone before and adds a new bit of action.

Part 3: Same team plays again as in Part 1, but with a new series of objects. This time, however, players take time to *see* each object as they listen.

Notes: 1. In Part 1 a player often will be able to remember every object or act in the series but, almost unbelievably, forgets the very last object named. Such a player has probably cut off his attention to the last player in order to pre-plan the object or act to be added.

2. However, when objects are acted out, players rarely forget preceding objects. Repeating Part 1 while *seeing* the objects named eases remembering for players.

Part 2: *Give objects their place in space!*
Keep objects in space — out of head!

Part 3: (As fellow players add new objects)
Take time to see the objects!
See the objects as they are added

Did you see the word as it was spoken?

—Singing Syllables——————————

Description: Players sit in a circle. One goes from the room and the others choose a word — for example, "Washington." The syllables of the word are distributed around the circle — "Wash" is given to the first group of players; "ing" to the second group, and "ton" to the third group so that all groups have an assigned syllable. To a familiar tune (such as "Yankee Doodle" or "Dixie") players sing their group's syllable over and over. The odd player walks about from group to group and tries to piece the word together, using as many guesses as needed. The game may be made more difficult by having players change places after the syllables have been given out, thus dispersing the groups. All groups sing their syllables to the same tune simultaneously.

More Where Games

See notes on Where, p. 30. Also see Verbalizing the Where, Parts 1 and 2, pp. 73-74.

—The Specialized Where————————

Purpose: To make the invisible setting visible.

Focus: On showing Where through the use of physical objects.

Description: Two or more players on a team. All teams are given the same general Where (a hotel room, an office, a schoolroom, etc.). Teams are to specialize the general Where (a hotel room *in Paris*, a *hospital* office, a *jungle* schoolroom) and choose Who and What .

Notes: 1. Encourage players to specialize the Where by making unusual choices (an office in Heaven; a jungle hotel room).
2. Sidecoach **Where with help!** and **Where with obstacles!** whenever the players need an assist.

Show! Don't tell!
Explore! Heighten!
Heighten the specific objects!

Did players choose distinctive objects that brought their specialized Where to life?
Or did they have to tell us Where they were through talking?
Players, do you agree?

WHAT TIME IS IT?

Purpose: To establish setting and environment.

Focus: On feeling time with the whole body, muscularly and kinesthetically.

Description: Count off into two large teams. Working individually, within the team, players sit or stand, focusing on a time of day given by the director. Players may move only if pushed to do so by the focus but are not to bring in activity just to show time.

Notes: 1. Players are not to interact with one another during this exercise.
2. Each player will feel the time differently. For instance, 2:00 a.m. will mean sleep for many, but the night owl in the group will become wide awake.
3. As in HOW OLD AM I? and WHAT DO I DO FOR A LIVING?, p. 87, repeat the time only and see what emerges.

Feel the time in your feet!
In your spine! In your legs!
No urgency!
Feel time on your face!
In your body!
Head to toe!
Allow the focus to work for you!

Is there bodily reaction to time?
Is it possible to communicate time without activity or objects?
Did everyone feel the time in his or her own way?
What were the differences?
Is clock time a cultural pattern?
Is there only sleep-time, work-time, hungry-time?

WHAT'S BEYOND: ACTIVITY

Purpose: To develop nonverbal communication.

Focus: On communicating activity in a place to be entered.

Description: One at a time, players enter, walk through the playing area, and exit. Without speech or unnecessary activity, player communicates what activity went on before the entrance or will take place after the exit.

Notes: 1. Keep evaluation on the focus only! We are not interested in anything but what has just happened or is about to happen.
2. If this exercise is given early, players should keep what happened simple (e.g., shoveling snow outside).
3. When repeated later, WHAT'S BEYOND could be based on relationships, such as a quarrel with a sweetheart, a funeral, a purse-snatching.

Show! Don't tell!
Let your body reflect what just took place!
Heighten it! Let your body reflect what activity will follow!

What had just happened?
Did player show or tell?
What will happen?
Did player show or tell?

──WHAT'S BEYOND?──────────────

Purpose: To communicate a past event and a present action simultaneously.

Focus: On what has happened in the beyond or what will happen, while totally involved in an onstage activity.

Description: Two or more players. Where, Who, and What agreed upon. Players are to pursue their activity (What) on stage. Thay have either done something together before they came on stage or are going to do something in the beyond when they leave.

Notes: 1. Have the What's Beyond be a *changed* event that deeply involves both players, e.g., a love affair, act of crime, death, divorce, playing hooky, loss of job. If What's Beyond is a simple shared offstage activity, the involvement (What's Between) will not energize onstage play.

2. Keep What's Beyond unrelated to what's happening on stage. It is not to be discussed between players nor is it to be suppressed. This seeming contradiction is what allows What's Beyond to burst through on the stage, a natural curtain results.

Involve yourself in the onstage activity!
Explore the space!
Heighten the connection!
Hold What's Beyond in no motion!
Fill the space with What's Beyond!

Did players stay with their focus or did they start acting!

Miscellaneous Games

——ADD A PART——

Purpose: To help players work together.

Focus: On using part of a whole object in space — out of the head.

Description: Eight to ten players per team. First player uses or makes contact with part of a larger object that only he or she has in mind and then leaves the playing area. One by one, players use or contact other parts of the whole object until the whole object is left in space.

Example: First player sits and uses a steering wheel, second wipes the windshield, third opens the car door, and so on.

Notes: 1. This game is similar to PART OF A WHOLE, p. 72, but players do not become the part with their bodies; rather they leave parts of a larger space object in the playing area.
2. Players are not to build their part of the object with tools, but by *using* that part. The windshield in the above example can be added by wiping its surface. The focus in this game is on the appearance — when the invisible becomes visible.

Let us see what you see!
Give the part its place in space!
Stay with the same whole object!
Other players see the whole through the parts left by others!
Avoid planning your part!
Use what was left by others and let your own part appear!

Audience, what was the complete object?
Were the added parts in the space or in the players' heads?
Players, do you agree?
First player, was that the object you had in mind?

——DEAF AUDIENCE——

Purpose: To develop physical communication.

Focus: On communicating a scene to a deaf audience.

Description: Two or more players. Who, Where, and What agreed upon. Members of the audience plug up their ears while watching the scene. Players are to go through scene as they normally would, using both dialogue and action.

Notes: 1. By being audience, players realize the necessity for showing, not telling.
2. The lifelessness of a scene in which actors merely talk instead of playing becomes evident to the most resistant.

Variation: Have audience close eyes instead of plugging ears.

Communicate!
Physicalize!
Show us!

Did the scene have animation?
Did you know what was going on, even though you could not hear them?
Where could they have physicalized the scene?

—BLIND——————————————————

Purpose: To develop full-body sensory awareness.

Focus: On moving about the playing area, while blind-folded, as if one could see, without groping.

Description: Two or more players prepare a simple Where, Who, and What and set up the playing area with real hand props, set pieces, chairs and tables. Playing area should be flat, with all sharp, pointed objects removed. Real prop blindfolds are needed. The What (activity) is to be one that requires handling and passing many objects, such as a tea party.

Notes: 1. In the beginning, loss of sight produces anxiety in some players, who stay immobilized in one spot. Sidecoaching and use of a prop telephone will help. Ring the bell (vocally if necessary) to call the player (by name) to the phone. It is not necessary to converse. Player will carry on.
2. Contact through handing around real props is necessary to the success of this exercise.

Follow through on that move!
Find the chair you were looking for!
Be adventurous!
Hang up your hat!
Integrate that groping into your character!

Did players move naturally?
Were all gropings integrated into the Where, Who, and What?
Was this integration interesting?
(If a player is looking for a chair, he or she might swing an arm or lurch as if such moves were part of the character.)

—PITCHMAN——————————————————

Purpose: To break down barriers between players and audience.

Focus: On communicating with the audience.

Description: Single player. The player must sell or demonstrate something to the audience. After going through a speech once, player is asked to repeat it again, but this time to *pitch* it.

Notes: 1. See GIBBERISH: SELLING, p. 53.
2. The player audience will recognize that a pitchman has to communicate with the audience and must therefore keep closely involved with them.

Pitch to us!
Heighten!
Stronger!

What was the difference between the two speeches?
Why did the pitching make the player come to life?

OCCLUDING

Purpose: To understand consciousness.

Focus: On occluding the subject, the Where, the character, fellow players, as sidecoached.

Description: Occluding (shutting in or out) does not mean ignoring what you are occluding. The player fully stays with whatever occluding is sidecoached, while at the same time embracing it.

Notes: 1. OCCLUDING, like many other games, is a paradox: the brain trying to figure out how to be aware of that which must be occluded. This produces a magical off-balance moment, one of the gateways into the intuitive.

2. The player's mind is emptied (free) of all manifestations of attitude or interpretations. This emptying allows energies to flow into and become part of what is *actually* happening. The invisible becomes visible.

3. What we are trying to make happen is the acceptance of the invisible as a probability for connection between players and audience, connection being the real communication.

4. A player in the pre-murder *Macbeth* scene, when sidecoached **Occlude Lady Macbeth!** became a most dangerous man, a passive man with a sword in his hand.

5. See TOUCH AND BE TOUCHED/SEE AND BE SEEN, p. 104.

Occlude the subject!
Occlude your fellow player!
Occlude the Where!

Glossary of Sidecoaching Phrases

All sidecoaching is given during playing and rehearsals. Actors do not stop to consider what is being sidecoached. They *act*! When sidecoaching begins to work for you and your cast, it is rarely realized as theatrical directing; a symbiotic connection results. Sidecoaching excites to action and hurtles everyone into the present.

Act! Don't react! Act goes forward; *react* is internalized before going out.

Allow the focus to work for you! Should *relax* player. Helps release obsessive control. An *outside force* is working and helping.

Contact! Vowels and consonants! Attitude! Spell! Reminders.

Expand that gesture! Pause! Widens experience.

Explore that object! Idea! Sound! Thought! Puts player into a meditative observation as exploration is sought.

Extend the sound! Reinforces movement, sight, thought, character.

Feel that! In your back! Feet! Head! Shoulders! An emotion takes over the whole body.

Give! Take! Take! Give! Awareness of others.

Give the ball (the word, the pause, the look) its time and space! A pause given. Time/space can be a very emotional stage moment. The same is true of a look, a word.

Gibberish! English! No time lag. No "should I or shouldn't I?" Now! Off-balance is built in. No time to think.

Heighten that moment . . . that feeling! Brings a brighter, broader, intensified experience.

Help your fellow player who isn't playing! Awakens cast to others' needs. Produces much stage business.

Keep your eye on the ball! Your fellow player! Your prop! Anchors player in movement.

Let your sight flow through your eyes! Let the sound flow through your ears! Let your mind flow through your brain! Useful for SPACE WALKS.

No motion! Stops excessive head control. Puts action and thought on a back burner.

Occlude your fellow player! Occlude the Where! Occlude the audience! Gives a new relation with the occluded; adds sight by bringing the occluded into sharp focus, as in a closeup; keeps a player from hiding. Can bring out hidden character qualities.

Out of your head, into the space! Open for the communication! Useful to get rid of attitudes. Players move out into the stage space. Frees the intuition (X-area).

Physicalize that thought! Gives physical (body) expression to a budding, emerging emotion.

See! Allow yourself to be seen! Come out, come out, wherever you are.

See the ceiling! The walls! Look out the window! Awakens the actor to the Where.

Share the space between you! Meet in the middle. The between space is where the individual energies can meet. Produces artistic detachment, makes visible to the players what is happening in regard to character and emotion.

Share your voice! Produces projection, responsibility to the audience. Not simply a direction to speak louder, it helps to alert a player organically, without the need for a lecture, to the need for personal interaction with the audience.

Slow Motion! Brings players into the moment of their playing. Details become sharpened. Players see and feel what is going on.

Stage picture! Helps players to see audience view. Brings players and audience into the stage space.

Stage whisper! Reminds players to whisper audibly. Intensifies relationships.

Stay out of it! Stops interfering. Stops controls.

Take a ride on your own body! View the scenery! Creates great artistic detachment. Useful during rehearsals.

Touch! Allow yourself to be touched! Expands the sensual world.

Two scenes! Two centers; clears confusion.

Use your whole body! Helps to physicalize emotions, feelings, thoughts, character.

You name it! You supply your own sidecoaching.

INDEX TO GAMES